Praise

Most leadership development books offer context-free surface-level advice. Dr. Sellers takes us into the real challenge: leading in the age of AI. With case studies and research, he shows that emotional intelligence isn't soft—it's essential. This book demands reflection and action. You won't read it without rethinking how you lead and shape future leaders in a rapidly changing world.

—Dr. Nigel Paine, Author of *The Great Reset and Workplace Learning*

In a world racing to adopt AI, Dr. Mikah Sellers brings us back to something timeless: the human core of leadership. This book is both deeply researched and refreshingly clear-eyed about what it takes to develop emotionally intelligent leaders. For L&D professionals, it's an invitation to move from ticking boxes to genuinely reshaping mindsets.

—Dr. Raghu Krishnamoorthy, Senior Fellow and Director,
Penn CLO Program; Former Chief Human Resources Officer, GE

This book is a bold, insightful guide to what truly drives leadership transformation. Dr. Sellers moves us beyond traditional leadership training to immersive, human-centered development, designed to equip leaders for the complex challenges of the AI era. A must-read for L&D professionals shaping the future of leadership.

—Dr. Keith Keating, Author of *Hidden Value*;
Chief L&D Officer, BDO

AI is already here, reshaping our work and our decisions. But for all it can do, it still can't listen, reassure, or build trust. That's where emotionally intelligent leadership comes in—and it's no longer optional. Dr. Sellers challenges us to audit our leadership programs and move emotional intelligence from the margins to the center. This book is both a wake-up call and a guide for anyone committed to helping leaders grow with integrity in the age of AI disruption. Our people—and our future—depend on it.

—Dr. Carmen M. Allison, Chief HR and Business Enablement Officer, Hoover Institution, Stanford University

Forging Emotionally Intelligent Leaders in the Age of AI

The Blueprint for Unlocking Human
Potential in the Future of Work

DR. MIKAH SELLERS

Foreword by Annie McKee

ISBN: 979-8-89079-346-1 (ebook)
ISBN: 979-8-89079-345-4 (paperback)
ISBN: 979-8-89079-344-7 (hardback)

Table of Contents

Part I:
Why Emotional Intelligence Is the Leadership Imperative

Part II:
How to Design for Transformational Growth

Part III:
Scaling Emotional Intelligence Across Systems

Appendices

Foreword

ANNIE MCKEE, PHD

In the early days of my research on emotional intelligence and leadership, I often encountered a particular kind of skepticism. "Emotions at work?" executives would ask, eyebrows raised. "Isn't that a bit... soft?"

Those days feel like a distant memory now. Today, as artificial intelligence reshapes every corner of our working lives, the question isn't whether emotions belong at work—it's whether we'll have the emotional intelligence to remain human in an increasingly automated world.

Dr. Mikah Sellers has written the book we need for this moment. In *Forging Emotionally Intelligent Leaders in the Age of AI*, he doesn't just make the case for emotional intelligence—he provides a comprehensive blueprint for cultivating it when the stakes have never been higher.

I've spent decades studying what makes leaders truly effective, and I've learned this: technical competence gets you in the door, but emotional intelligence determines whether you'll succeed once you're there. This truth becomes even more pronounced in our AI-driven era. As machines handle more of our analytical work, our uniquely human capacities—empathy, moral reasoning, the ability to inspire trust in uncertain times—become our greatest competitive advantage.

What strikes me most about Dr. Sellers' approach is his deep understanding that developing emotional intelligence isn't about downloading new content into leaders' minds. Real transformation happens through experience, reflection, and authentic human connection. His original research—drawn from extensive fieldwork with senior executives who participated in immersive, multi-week leadership development programs—reveals something I've long believed: we don't just teach people to be emotionally intelligent—we create the conditions where their emotional intelligence can emerge and flourish.

The immersive, experience-based programs Dr. Sellers studied and describes in this book mirror what I've witnessed in my own work with leaders around the world. The most profound breakthroughs don't happen in conference rooms filled with PowerPoint presentations. They happen when leaders feel safe enough to be vulnerable, when they're challenged to examine their deepest assumptions, and when they're supported by peers who see both their struggles and their potential. Dr. Sellers' research provides compelling evidence for what many of us have intuited: transformation requires more than information transfer—it demands emotional engagement, sustained duration, and carefully crafted experiences that touch identity itself.

This book arrives at a critical juncture. As AI eliminates routine tasks and accelerates decision-making, leaders face unprecedented moral complexity. Should we deploy an algorithm that improves efficiency but might perpetuate bias? How do we communicate layoffs driven by automation with honesty and compassion? Who bears responsibility when machine learning models cause harm? These aren't technical questions—they're fundamentally human ones that require emotional intelligence, ethical clarity, and moral courage.

Dr. Sellers understands that preparing leaders for this reality requires more than updating our curriculum—it demands transforming how we think about leadership development itself. His framework moves us beyond the traditional training-as-transfer model toward something far more powerful: learning as transformation. This shift isn't just pedagogically sound; it's essential for developing the kind of leaders our organizations and society need.

What you'll find in these pages isn't another collection of frameworks or assessment tools. Instead, Dr. Sellers offers something rarer and more valuable: a research-informed approach to creating experiences that change people at their core. His work shows us how to design programs that don't just inform leaders about emotional intelligence— they help leaders become more emotionally intelligent human beings.

The journey from information to transformation isn't easy. It requires courage from both learners and facilitators. It demands that we create psychological safety while also inviting stretch and challenge. It asks us to value depth over efficiency and meaning over metrics. But as Dr. Sellers demonstrates through compelling research and vivid stories, this journey is worth taking.

As I read about the leaders who participated in his research—executives who learned to lead with vulnerability rather than control, who discovered how to remain grounded amid chaos, who found ways to build trust across differences—I was reminded of why this work matters so profoundly. These aren't just better leaders; they're better humans. And in a world where AI can replicate many of our cognitive abilities, our humanity becomes our greatest gift.

The future doesn't need more efficient leaders or smarter algorithms. It needs wise leaders who can navigate complexity with emotional intelligence, who can make ethical decisions under pressure, and who can inspire others to bring their full humanity to work. Dr. Sellers has given us a valuable guide for developing exactly these kinds of leaders.

I encourage you to read this book not just with your mind, but with your heart. Notice where it challenges your assumptions. Pay attention to the moments that make you uncomfortable—they're often the most important ones. And most importantly, use what you learn to create the kinds of transformational experiences that will forge the emotionally intelligent leaders our world needs.

The future of work is being written now. Let's make sure it's a profoundly human story.

Annie McKee, PhD
Author of *How to Be Happy at Work;* Co-author with Daniel Goleman and Richard Boyatzis of *Primal Leadership;* co-author of *Resonant Leadership* and *How to Become a Resonant Leader*

Introduction

What if the most critical leadership skills in the age of AI aren't technical at all, but deeply human?

As a new wave of technological innovation driven by AI and automation reshapes the workplace and absorbs more knowledge work, one truth becomes clear: tomorrow's most effective leaders will be those who lead with emotional intelligence. They'll foster trust, navigate ambiguity, and inspire teams with courage and compassion.

This book doesn't attempt to define or redefine emotional intelligence. That work has already been done—brilliantly—by Daniel Goleman, Richard Boyatzis, Annie McKee, and others. *Forging Emotionally Intelligent Leaders in the Age of AI* is something else: a blueprint for designing transformational programs that develop emotionally intelligent leaders, especially in a world where AI and automation are rapidly transforming the nature of knowledge work and leadership.

Why Emotional Intelligence Is the AI Era's Human Advantage

In the early days of my doctoral research, I sat with a senior executive who had just completed a multi-week immersive leadership program. She had led global teams through mergers, pivots, and crises. But this moment was different. "I've never had to lead through this much uncertainty. It's not just the pace of change—it's the emotional toll it's taking on people. And I don't think we're ready for what's coming."

Her words stayed with me, not because they were rare, but because I heard them again and again in nearly every interview. Senior executives weren't looking for another framework. They were craving steadiness, the emotional capacity to lead through chaos, ambiguity, and disruption.

We are living through a profound turning point. AI isn't just changing how work gets done—it's changing how leadership must be practiced.

AI can now draft legal contracts, generate code, compose marketing campaigns, personalize customer experiences, detect fraud, diagnose diseases, and analyze millions of data points in seconds. It powers autonomous systems, accelerates innovation pipelines, optimizes supply chains, and augments decision-making across every function of the enterprise. It's fast, tireless, and rapidly taking on other sophisticated knowledge work.

However, it still can't do what leadership truly requires: build trust, create meaning in the midst of ambiguity, foster psychological safety, resolve human conflict, or inspire people toward a shared purpose. That remains uniquely human. And it's not just our responsibility—it's our greatest opportunity.

The Human Edge

The core argument of this book is this: as automation reshapes the nature of work, emotionally intelligent leadership has become essential, not just for navigating disruption, but for sustaining trust, inclusion, and human connection. But cultivating that kind of leadership demands more than information. It calls for immersive, identity-level transformation.

In my research of immersive, multi-week executive education programs focused on developing emotional intelligence, the breakthroughs that mattered didn't happen in slide decks or lectures. They happened in emotional exercises, in moments of reflection after failure or conflict, and in courageous peer dialogue. Leaders weren't changed by information. They were changed by experience, especially those that touched their values, fears, and sense of identity.

Fewer than 30% of participants had received any prior formal training in emotional intelligence. Yet, more than 85% pointed to emotionally charged moments, like receiving feedback, sharing a personal story, or facing an ethical dilemma, as the most transformative parts of their journey.

As one executive reflected:

"No one ever taught me how to be with emotion—mine or anyone else's. Once I learned to do that, everything changed. I became more human. And oddly, more effective."

This is not a side note. That is the work.

Why Now

We are not going through a period of change. We are living in a state of continuous disruption. Technology is outpacing human adaptation. Organizations are under pressure to innovate, adapt, and perform all at once. Leaders can't simply manage the chaos—they must help people make sense of it and navigate through it.

In this climate, emotionally intelligent leaders are not just effective—they are essential to:

- Guide teams through fear and resistance to change.
- Cultivate psychological safety that fuels innovation.

- Interpret algorithmic decisions with ethical clarity.

- Build cultures of trust, resilience, and inclusion.

- Hold space for grief, tension, and transformation.

The World Economic Forum's 2023 Future of Jobs Report lists emotional intelligence among the top 10 competencies for the evolving workforce. McKinsey's *State of Organizations* report highlights adaptability, empathy, and ethics as "mission-critical" for modern leadership.

The takeaway is clear: emotional intelligence is not a soft skill for leaders in the Age of AI—it's a strategic one.

What This Book Offers

This book makes the case that effective leadership development requires more than just content delivery. It requires emotional engagement, immersive experiences, psychological safety, emotional activation, and peer-driven learning to create the conditions for lasting transformation. It argues that leadership development must move beyond content delivery. We need experiences that engage the whole person—head, heart, and habit.

Drawing from original research, two decades of executive experience, and firsthand stories of transformation, this book reveals what works when it comes to transformative leadership development:

- Safe containers for vulnerability, reflection, and feedback

- Immersive experiences that challenge identity

- Peer dynamics that foster accountability and connection

- Coaching that sustains learning and transformation

- Organizational strategies that align EI with ways of working and culture

- T&D functions that drive enterprise agility by developing emotionally intelligent leaders and shaping a culture of EI-driven norms

Each chapter explores these ideas through narrative, data, and design principles that you can apply.

A Note on the Research

The findings in this book stem from my doctoral dissertation and follow-up fieldwork, which involved in-depth interviews with senior executives who participated in immersive, multi-week leadership development programs designed to foster the development of emotional intelligence competencies.

Throughout the book, you'll find "Research Spotlights" and stories that illuminate insights from that work. These stories have been anonymized and presented as composites to protect the confidentiality of study participants. They aren't fictional. They are lived accounts, rendered with clarity and care to illuminate the pathways of transformation.

Who This Book Is For

If you're a talent and development (T&D) executive, senior organizational transformation leader, HR strategist, or executive coach looking to evolve your leadership development efforts, this book is for you. It's for those ready to move beyond check-the-box training and toward programs that reshape who leaders are as people and how they lead.

You'll find:

- A critique of outdated leadership development models

- A research-informed framework for designing and delivering leadership development training programs that transform rather than inform

- Practical exercises and program designs you can adapt

- A call to embed emotional intelligence into the organizational operating system and culture

Why This Matters Now

AI is changing what we do. Emotional intelligence will determine how we do it—and how well we guide others through the uncertainty and workplace transformation it brings.

The leaders of tomorrow won't just be those who keep up with change. They'll be the ones who stay grounded, connected, and clear when the future is anything but.

And that kind of leadership isn't taught in one-off, short-term training programs. It's forged through experience, reflection, feedback, and honest community.

That's the journey this book invites you to take.

Let's begin.

PART I

Why Emotional Intelligence Is
the Leadership Imperative

1

The Moral Frontier of Leadership in the Age of AI

The Challenge Is Human

When a rising leader at a fintech company was asked how she planned to roll out an AI-driven risk model expected to reduce headcount by 15%, she didn't begin with the algorithm. She started with her people.

"I know the model works," she said. "The harder question is—how do I do this in a way that doesn't break trust?"

That question reflects a deeper shift underway.

AI isn't on the horizon. It's already here, shaping the everyday decisions leaders make—prioritizing sales leads, forecasting revenue, interpreting employee sentiment, resolving support tickets, and synthesizing market trends. It manages inventory, automates compliance, and even assists in product design.

What was once a technical conversation has become a deeply human one. Leading in the age of AI demands more than logic. It calls for empathy, ethics, and emotional courage.

Again and again, senior leaders told me: the toughest choices today aren't about what AI can do. They're about what we should do with it.

AI can surface insights, flag issues, and cut costs. But it can't build trust. It can't lead challenging conversations with empathy. It can't preserve psychological safety when the pressure is high.

That responsibility still falls to us. And it may be our most crucial job.

Beyond Efficiency: The Ethical Complexity AI Introduces

Every day, leaders are making decisions about AI that aren't just strategic—they're moral.

- Should we use a model that improves speed but risks repeating historical bias?

- Can we automate roles without offering reskilling?

- How do we talk about layoffs—with honesty or corporate spin?

- Who is accountable when a machine learning model causes harm?

These are more than technical questions. They test our relationships, emotions, and values.

A global health executive I interviewed shared the moment his AI triage system led to a round of layoffs. When asked about the human cost, he said, "The numbers were right. The ethics were less clear."

Emotionally intelligent leadership doesn't promise easy answers. It offers the capacity to tackle tough ones with integrity.

In a world optimized for efficiency, emotional intelligence becomes an ethical enabler.

It helps leaders:

- **Stay aware** when fear, ego, or urgency cloud judgment.
- **Feel what others feel**, so decisions aren't made in a vacuum.
- **Regulate emotion** in moments of discomfort, rather than rushing to the most politically safe solution.
- **Sense what's unsaid**—the tension, hesitation, or distrust within a team or stakeholder group.
- **Voice concerns and hold boundaries** when values are at stake.

These aren't soft skills. They're the foundation of trust, ethical reasoning, and human-centered decision-making.

When AI creates a gray zone between what's possible and what's right, emotionally intelligent leaders are the moral anchors. They ask:

- Who might this harm?
- What assumptions are we embedding?
- Where might silence be complicity?
- Could I defend this decision to my team, my family, or myself?

What Makes This Challenge Different

For decades, leadership development focused on driving performance and efficiency. Emotional intelligence and ethical discernment were rarely at the forefront of the agenda.

That mindset no longer works.

AI and automation are reshaping industries—and the emotional landscape of work. Employees feel real anxiety about being replaced, deskilled, or depersonalized.

According to Pew Research (2023), 62% of U.S. workers expect AI to have a significant impact on the workforce, and 32% fear job loss. The stress is real. So is the distrust.

Executives are also under pressure, navigating a complex web of innovation, reputational risk, workforce well-being, and regulatory ambiguity.

- Should we use generative AI for customer service, even if it erodes human connection?
- Can we automate roles that serve vulnerable populations?
- Who's responsible when an algorithm harms underrepresented groups?

These decisions have ripple effects on people, culture, trust, and brand loyalty.

And customers are watching. A Deloitte study found that 57% of consumers are more loyal to companies that address the ethical risks of new technology. One misstep with AI, and trust can erode overnight.

This isn't a moment of temporary change. This is a structural transformation. Leading through it requires a new kind of leadership—emotionally intelligent, ethically grounded, and unapologetically human.

Emotional Intelligence as a Leadership Advantage

In this era of disruption, emotional intelligence isn't a bonus—it's a necessity.

It gives leaders the internal stability to navigate external volatility. It enables them to connect, make decisions, and lead when the stakes are high and the answers are unclear.

Leaders with strong emotional intelligence can:

- Pause before reacting under pressure

- Identify fear, grief, or resistance in a room, and respond with empathy

- Speak honestly when trust is fragile

- Stay anchored in their values—even when performance metrics tempt them to compromise

- Build psychological safety, so people feel seen, heard, and safe enough to adapt

Emotional intelligence accounts for up to 90% of the difference between top-performing and average leaders (Harvard Business Review, 2017). According to Six Seconds (2021), teams led by high-EI managers report four times higher engagement and dramatically lower burnout.

EI isn't just about managing people. It's about leading with clarity, connection, and conscience.

It's the bridge between innovation and integrity.

Research Spotlight

In my research, leaders emphasized the pivotal role EI played in high-stakes moments: "We were implementing a powerful AI tool. Technically, it worked. But the rollout would have failed without the human component—listening to concerns, being honest about trade-offs, and holding space for anxiety and resistance."

Leaders often described how emotional intelligence influenced their daily decisions, fostered trust, and sustained momentum during transformation.

Case Studies from the Frontlines

Reworking Algorithmic Bias

A fintech firm discovered its credit model was unintentionally rejecting applicants from underrepresented communities. An emotionally intelligent leader paused the launch, built a diverse cross-functional team, and invited affected customers into the process. The result? A fairer model—and renewed trust.

Communicating Displacement with Dignity

When a health system automated several diagnostic roles, the COO didn't issue cold notices. She hosted live forums, provided coaching, and developed customized reskilling plans. The transition wasn't easy. But it was human, and employees remembered that.

Inclusive AI Implementation

At a logistics company, the initial rollout of a scheduling AI failed because it didn't account for Spanish-speaking workers. Mistrust spread quickly. A frontline operations leader stepped in, offered bilingual training, reopened communication channels, and collaborated across functions to adjust the rollout. Adoption rebounded.

Moral Reasoning in the Machine Age

The most consequential decisions of this era won't come from code. They'll come from humans choosing how to use it.

And those choices will often be emotionally and ethically complex.

In my research, the most effective leaders didn't just know what to do—they knew how to pause, feel, and choose. They:

- Stayed present in ambiguity
- Treated resistance as a signal, not a threat
- Modeled empathy and clarity in tense moments
- Asked hard questions and listened for discomfort
- Stayed rooted in values—even when it hurt

One leader put it plainly: "My job isn't to predict the future. It's to lead through it with integrity."

Emotional intelligence isn't just a leadership skill—it's a compass. It keeps leaders human, especially when the incentives tempt them to lose sight of their humanity.

What This Means for Leadership Development

To prepare leaders for the AI era, T&D must go beyond upskilling. We must help leaders:

- **Reflect on values**, not just repeat rules

- **Rehearse real-world ethical tension**, not just discuss theory

- **Respond to resistance with emotional agility**, not control

- **Build moral courage** through lived experience, not slide decks

This means integrating emotional intelligence into the heart of your leadership curriculum, not as an optional module, but at the core of every aspect of your programs.

Opportunity for Reflection

Reflect on a decision that involved AI, automation, or rapid change.

- What emotional or ethical tension did it raise?

- How did you navigate it, and what shaped your response?

- How might emotional intelligence have helped, or did it already?

Practice for T&D Leaders

Conduct an EI audit. Look at your current leadership programs. Where is emotional intelligence assumed, but not explicitly developed?

Then ask:

- Are leaders practicing moral decision-making under pressure?

- Are we teaching self-awareness as rigorously as strategy?

- Do we model empathy in our own facilitation and feedback loops?

Elevate emotional intelligence from the margins to the center. In the age of AI, human capacity will be the most valuable form of intelligence we possess.

A Transition to What's Next

We've seen why emotionally intelligent leadership is no longer optional. Now, let's look more closely at what today's leaders are up against—and why feeling more deeply may be the only way to lead wisely when machines think faster than we do.

2

When Machines Think Faster, Leaders Must Feel Deeper

The Moment It Changed

Jasmin had always been ahead of the curve. As VP of Operations at a global logistics firm, she led with precision, speed, and the confidence of someone who had seen around corners before.

When her company adopted an AI system that automated nearly 30% of her team's tasks, she focused on the mechanics, systems integration, process redesign, and resource allocation. Every metric was accounted for.

Except one: emotional impact.

During a tense project review, a senior analyst turned to her and asked, "Do I still matter here?"

Jasmin froze. The dashboards didn't cover that. The strategic plan had no chapter on fear.

What she said next wasn't in the playbook. It was real. "You do. But how you matter will need to evolve."

That moment marked a shift, not just for her team but for Jasmin as a leader. She realized that leadership in the age of AI wasn't just about mastering new tools. It was about meeting people where they were.

This is the threshold we now face.
A New Leadership Threshold

AI is no longer theoretical. It's writing job descriptions, forecasting demand, drafting reports, and analyzing patterns faster than any human team. For knowledge workers, disruption isn't looming—it's here.

And yet, for all AI can do, it still cannot:

- Rebuild trust when teams feel insecure
- Offer empathy in a performance review
- Sit with moral discomfort and choose integrity
- Help a team find meaning after roles shift
- Listen, reassure, or lead with presence

As AI accelerates execution, leadership must deepen connection at all levels. What matters now isn't how much you know, but how well you lead when the human stakes are high.

The Great Decoupling:
Tasks vs. Capabilities

For generations, leadership was measured by execution. You got promoted for doing more, knowing more, and managing more resources and initiatives.

The rules are changing.

AI can now perform many of the core tasks we once called leadership, analyzing data, synthesizing complex information, and generating insights that can be translated into actionable strategies. What it cannot do is hold emotional space for a fearful team. It can't resolve ethical tension. It can't mentor someone through reinvention.

This is the Great Decoupling: tasks and capabilities are splitting apart. The ability to perform tasks is no longer what defines a leader. Human capacity—emotional intelligence, relational judgment, and moral courage—is what will distinguish the great from the good.

As AI scales knowledge, leaders must scale wisdom. Wisdom work means leading not just with knowledge, but with clarity, care, and conviction when there's no clear answer, especially when automation collides with human values.

What AI Excels At	What Human Leaders Must Excel At
Processing and analyzing vast data sets	Navigating ambiguity with emotional steadiness
Writing reports, code, and generating content	Inspiring and aligning diverse teams
Predicting outcomes with probabilistic models	Making values-based decisions under ethical complexity

| Automating routine and complex tasks | Building trust during change and disruption |
| Operating at scale and speed | Leading inclusively across differences |

This contrast highlights a critical truth: the future of leadership will hinge not on what leaders know, but on how they show up.

Redefining What Makes a Leader Great

The old model of leadership prized control, subject-matter expertise, and output. But in today's fast-moving, emotionally complex environments, those skills are necessary but not sufficient.

Today's best leaders:

- Communicate with empathy and transparency

- Regulate their emotions in high-pressure moments

- Make values-based decisions even when under scrutiny

- Translate complexity into direction and reassurance

- Foster trust across generational and cultural divides

According to McKinsey's *State of Organizations 2023*, the top leadership capabilities cited as critical to navigating disruption include adaptability, emotional intelligence, and ethical decision-making. The *World Economic Forum* confirms this, ranking emotional intelligence among the top ten essential skills for the future of work.

What this tells us: the leaders of tomorrow won't just be the most informed. They'll be the most emotionally equipped.

Research Spotlight: The Leadership Gap in the Age of Acceleration

In my study of immersive leadership programs focused on emotional intelligence, a pattern emerged: the real breakthroughs didn't come from lectures or frameworks.

They came from emotionally charged moments:

- Receiving raw feedback

- Confronting a blind spot

- Sharing a personal failure

- Feeling seen and accepted by peers

One executive put it this way: "It wasn't until I broke down sharing a personal leadership failure, and the group leaned in—not away—that I realized leadership isn't about being right. It's about being real."

Emotionally intelligent leadership doesn't emerge from knowledge. It emerges from experience.

Why Emotional Intelligence Matters More Now

AI excels at patterns. People don't. People feel fear. They resist. They get tired. They need meaning.

The more organizations rely on AI to generate insight, the more emotionally intelligent leaders must become to guide teams through change. Emotional intelligence becomes the counterbalance, what keeps the human heartbeat in the machine age.

It enables leaders to:

- Pause before reacting to friction or bad news
- Name and normalize anxiety without losing momentum
- Communicate clearly, even when the message is hard
- Stay anchored in values while navigating uncertainty
- Create team environments where ideas and emotions can coexist

In short, emotional intelligence helps leaders build trust in environments where trust is fragile.

Trust Is the New Currency

AI may power our systems, but trust is what powers our teams.

People don't follow leaders because they have the best ideas. They follow them because they feel safe, heard, and seen. Trust is built in moments, such as how a leader responds to criticism, whether they acknowledge uncertainty, and how they show up in conflict.

As one executive told me, "If my team doesn't trust me, it doesn't matter how good the plan is. They won't follow."

What this means for leaders: To lead effectively in an AI-driven world, you must demonstrate emotional consistency. Trust won't scale without your presence.

Wisdom Over Optimization

AI finds the statistically likely answer. Leadership requires the morally right one.

Emotionally intelligent leaders don't defer to what's easiest. They sense when something feels off. They stay in the discomfort long enough to ask, "Are we optimizing at the cost of our values?"

That's not softness. That's strength.

What this means for leaders: If your instinct says something's missing, listen. Numbers may clarify, but wisdom leads.

Resilience in a State of Perpetual Disruption

We're no longer preparing for disruption. We're living in it.

New technologies, social shifts, and economic uncertainty now define the landscape. And the leaders who thrive aren't the ones who can push through. They're the ones who can slow down, reset, and help others stay centered.

Resilient leaders don't ignore chaos. They learn to breathe inside of it.

What this means for leaders: Your emotional tone sets the temperature. Resilience is contagious—and it starts with you.

Innovation Requires Psychological Safety

Top-performing teams don't just have talent. They have safety.

Google's Project Aristotle confirmed what decades of research already showed: people take creative risks when they know they won't be punished for failing, asking, or questioning.

That climate is created by emotionally intelligent leadership—leaders who can read the room, defuse tension, and make space for new voices.

What this means for leaders: You can't have innovation without risk. And you can't have risk without safety. EI builds the conditions where ideas grow.

What This Means for Leadership Development

Leadership programs can no longer treat emotional intelligence as "nice to have." It's the skill set that makes all other capabilities work effectively under pressure.

To prepare leaders for AI-era complexity, T&D must help them build:

- **Self-Awareness:** Recognize emotional patterns and triggers
- **Self-Regulation:** Stay steady and grounded in stress
- **Empathy:** Understand others' experiences and needs
- **Organizational Awareness:** Read emotional currents across teams
- **Influence:** Earn trust and inspire action through authentic presence
- **Conflict Management:** Handle tension with emotional agility
- **Coaching & Mentoring:** Support team growth amid change
- **Teamwork:** Foster inclusion and belonging across boundaries

These are not "soft" skills. They are essential skills. And they must be practiced, not just understood.

Opportunity for Reflection

Recall a recent moment of disruption or high-stakes change in your team or organization.

- How were people's emotions, yours or others', recognized or overlooked?

- What did leaders do that helped build trust or, unintentionally, erode it?

- How might greater emotional self-awareness or a safer team environment have changed the outcome?

Emotional intelligence is most evident under pressure. Reflecting on those moments helps build the muscle to respond more intentionally in the future.

Practice for T&D Leaders

Facilitate a Leadership Roundtable on the Emotional Impact of AI. Convene a cross-functional roundtable with senior leaders—from operations, technology, HR, and strategy—to examine where AI and automation are creating emotional disruption within the organization. Focus the discussion around four key areas:

1. **Trust and Transparency**

    o   Where are teams experiencing uncertainty, confusion, or fear about AI-related changes?

    o   Are employees expressing concerns about fairness, job security, or lack of communication?

2. **Psychological Safety and Innovation**

    o   Are there signals that psychological safety is eroding (e.g., lower participation, idea withholding)?

o How are leaders creating—or unintentionally closing—space for open dialogue during change?

3. **Change Fatigue and Engagement**

o What trends are surfacing around disengagement, burn-out, or emotional withdrawal?

o Are managers equipped to sense and address these signs early?

4. **Values Alignment in Decision-Making**

o Where are decisions involving AI adoption conflicting with organizational values?

o Do leaders feel confident navigating those tensions with moral clarity?

Use the insights gathered to:

- **Diagnose Emotional Hot Spots**: Map areas of high emotional friction where AI disruption is most acute.

- **Prioritize Program Redesign**: Align leadership development curricula with the most urgent emotional intelligence capabilities, such as coaching during change, managing uncertainty, and ethical communication.

- **Design Experience-Based Learning Modules**: Develop scenario-based exercises that simulate emotionally complex decisions (e.g., restructuring due to AI, ethical dilemmas in automation, team communication post-deployment).

- **Measure Emotional Indicators**: Introduce pulse surveys, reflection tools, or qualitative check-ins that monitor team trust, psychological safety, and perceived fairness before and after AI-related shifts.

By embedding emotional awareness into both program design and performance outcomes, talent and development (T&D) leaders shift from reactive support to strategic foresight, enabling the organization to build resilience, retain talent, and navigate transformation with humanity at its center.

A Call to Talent & Development Leaders

This moment isn't just an opportunity for talent and development leaders—it's a turning point.

As transformation accelerates, T&D must ensure leadership programs cultivate the emotional intelligence competencies that help leaders navigate the seismic shifts AI is driving across the workplace.

The most impactful programs will develop leaders with the emotional capacity to face uncertainty, respond with integrity, and make the most human decisions amid disruption, ambiguity, and accelerating change.

T&D professionals who embrace this shift won't just support strategy—they'll shape it. They'll become builders of culture, catalysts for transformation, and stewards of human work.

A Transition to What's Next

If emotional intelligence is so essential, why do most programs still struggle to teach it?

In the next chapter, we'll explore why traditional leadership development often fails—and what it takes to design experiences that lead to real change.

3

The Problem With Traditional Leadership Development

The Training That Didn't Work

D aniel was brilliant. Engineering degree. MBA from a top-20 school. He managed a $400 million product portfolio and had just been promoted to lead a cross-functional innovation team at a global tech firm.

Three months in, the cracks began to show. His team was disengaged. Conflict festered. Anonymous feedback painted a troubling picture: "intense," "distant," "quick to dismiss."

In response, the company sent him to a high-end leadership development program. The curriculum promised to boost his "executive presence" and equip him to "lead through change."

It was polished. It was expensive. It was ineffective.

Daniel could recite the models. He aced the quizzes. But he couldn't pause before reacting. He couldn't sit with uncertainty without grasping for control. He couldn't build trust because he was leading from anxiety, not awareness.

The program taught him content. What he needed was transformation.

The Fallacy of Training-as-Transfer

Too many organizations treat leadership development like data transfer: deliver tools, check comprehension, and expect new behavior.

This approach rests on flawed assumptions:

- Knowledge = Capability
- Exposure = Integration
- Attendance = Transformation

But adult learning doesn't follow this formula. Growth isn't a transaction. It's a process—emotional, contextual, and identity-based.

According to transformative learning theory (Mezirow, 1997), adults change when they confront disorienting experiences that challenge their assumptions and catalyze shifts in perspective. In other words, change comes from the inside out, not just from the outside in.

Leaders don't grow because they've been taught about empathy. They develop when they experience emotional tension, reflect on their beliefs, and choose new responses that align with who they want to become.

Why Traditional Programs Fall Short

1. They Ignore How Adults Really Learn

Most programs rely on passive delivery: lectures, slide decks, videos. These transfer information, but not insight.

But adult learners crave:

- **Autonomy** in their learning

- **Emotional relevance** tied to real work

- **Practical application** of ideas

- **Safe stretch experiences** that push edges without overwhelm

As Knowles' principles of andragogy emphasize, adults learn best when learning is self-directed, experience-based, and immediately applicable. When these are missing, learning can fade quickly.

2. They Focus on Performance, Not Identity

Many programs train behaviors, such as communication tips, influence tactics, and conflict styles. But behavior change without identity work is temporary.

Leadership isn't just what you do. It's who you are while doing it.

Daniel could perform. But his urge to control stemmed from fear—fear of being irrelevant, wrong, or dismissed. Until he surfaced those beliefs, his behavior wouldn't change where it counted.

Transformative learning occurs when programs invite leaders to explore not only how they act, but also why.

3. They Underestimate Emotion

Too often, emotion is seen as noise in leadership development—something to manage or ignore. But it's the signal.

Emotion is what gives learning weight. Cherniss and Goleman noted that "to engage the emotional circuitry is to increase the chances of behavior change."

The most memorable, meaningful leadership lessons are rarely delivered in perfect lighting on stage. They happen in discomfort, in reflection, in real moments of vulnerability.

Effective programs lean into this. They create experiences where leaders:

- Share failure stories
- Name fear, shame, or doubt
- Practice giving and receiving honest feedback
- Are seen fully, and still accepted

Emotion isn't a barrier to learning. It's the gateway.

4. They Confuse Exposure with Integration

One keynote on psychological safety doesn't make a team safe. A slide on trust doesn't make a leader trustworthy.

Exposure creates awareness, but that's not the same as development. True growth requires:

- **Practice over time**
- **Ongoing reflection**
- **Behavioral feedback loops**
- **Facilitated conversations** that deepen insight

One leader put it bluntly: "We had a great session on EI. Then we moved on. No space to apply it. No time to make it real."

Without integration, learning becomes noise—impressive but ineffective.

Research Spotlight: Identity, Emotion, and Deep Learning

In my research, leaders who experienced the most growth didn't cite models or slide decks. They pointed to emotional turning points that reshaped their self-perception.

One reflected: "I realized the way I managed conflict came from how I protected myself growing up. That insight changed everything."

Another said: "The moment I told my story—and was still accepted— was when I felt safe enough to change."

These were not the results of passive content delivery. They emerged from learning environments that balanced psychological safety with challenge, invited emotional engagement, and encouraged reflection.

These programs weren't just events. They were experiences—carefully designed to shift not just behavior, but identity.

A Call to T&D: Redesign the Architecture

If today's challenges are emotional, ambiguous, and identity-based, our learning designs must meet them head-on.

The best programs I studied followed a clear formula:

Immersion × (Psychological Safety + Stretch Challenge) + Emotion + Structured Reflection = Lasting Transformation

This means designing for:

- **Emotional activation** (not emotional avoidance)
- **Safe vulnerability** (not superficial dialogue)
- **Time to metabolize learning** (not just check completion)

In short, T&D must evolve from curriculum design to transformation design.

What This Means for Leadership Development

Here's what transformation-ready design looks like:

- **From content to experience:** Replace passive sessions with immersive storytelling, peer dialogue, and emotional engagement.

- **From frameworks to feelings:** Help leaders surface emotions and beliefs—not just memorize models.

- **From exposure to integration:** Develop multi-touch, longitudinal programs that incorporate space for practice, application, and coaching.

- **From safe to stretching:** Create space for truth-telling and challenge, without sacrificing psychological safety.

This is not about discarding content. It's about designing programs that actually lead to change.

Opportunity for Reflection

Think back to a leadership development experience you've delivered— or participated in:

- What moment truly challenged someone's sense of self?

- Where did participants move from information to insight?

- What would you redesign to create more depth, safety, or emotional impact?

Practice for T&D Leaders

To shift from content delivery to transformation design, try this:

Design an "Inside-Out" Session:
Replace one presentation-heavy session in your leadership develop-
ment program with a facilitated, emotionally grounded experience.
Choose from:

- **Storytelling Circles:** Invite participants to share moments of
  failure, challenge, or fear, and what they learned.

- **Identity Mapping:** Have leaders trace their values and forma-
  tive experiences to understand what drives them.

- **Empathy Dialogues:** Pair participants to share a current
  work struggle, with partners practicing deep listening and reflection.

Then build a structured debrief:

- What surfaced?

- What surprised you?

- How does this shape how you lead?

Finally, follow up with reflection prompts and peer coaching touchpoints. This is how we build integration, not just exposure.

A Transition to What's Next

If most programs fail to create lasting change, what does transformation actually look like?

In the next chapter, we'll explore what happens in the brain during
meaningful learning—and how the right design can trigger new

neural pathways, new behaviors, and new ways of being. You'll meet a high-performing leader whose breakthrough didn't come from knowing more, but from feeling more.

4

The Neuroscience of Leadership Transformation

The Leader Who Rewired

Melissa was the kind of leader most companies want more of. A senior executive at a global consumer goods firm, she was known for delivering results. Her track record was clean. Her team hit every metric. Her performance reviews were glowing.

But her 360° feedback told a different story:

- "She doesn't really listen."

- "If you disagree, she shuts it down."

- "You never know what she actually feels."

Melissa equated emotional control with strength. Under pressure, she tightened her grip on decisions, on people, on herself. She thought she was being composed. In truth, she was leading from fear.

When she entered a multi-week immersive leadership program, she came with a checklist mentality: take notes, complete the modules, return stronger.

What she didn't expect was the moment she finally let down her guard.

During a peer storytelling exercise, Melissa shared the personal loss of her sister. Something shifted. Her voice cracked. She paused. Her teammates leaned in.

Later, she reflected, "I didn't realize how much of my leadership was about not feeling anything at all."

That moment wasn't just powerful. It was transformational. Melissa didn't just learn something—she changed. Not because she was told what to do, but because the experience struck her at her emotional core.

What Traditional Programs Miss: The Brain's Resistance to Change

Leadership programs often focus on logic, strategy, and frameworks. But under pressure, leaders don't default to knowledge—they default to instinct.

The emotional brain, not the rational brain, takes the lead when stress strikes. Without deliberate practice and emotional safety, even the most well-meaning leaders revert to habits:

- Control over curiosity

- Avoidance over presence

- Defensiveness over reflection

Neuroscience confirms it: change that sticks must reach the limbic system, where habits, emotional memory, and identity reside. That requires more than content. It demands emotional engagement and repetition in psychologically safe environments.

The Science of Learning: Transformation Is Neurobiological

Most leadership development programs assume insight leads to action. However, change isn't just cognitive—it's embodied. The prefrontal cortex governs logic and planning. That's where most training focuses.

But lasting transformation lives in the limbic system—the emotional brain, where habits, memories, and motivation are stored.

Brain Region	Function	Implication for Leadership Learning
Prefrontal Cortex	Logic, planning, analysis	Supports intellectual understanding of concepts
Limbic System	Emotion, memory, motivation, behavior	Drives long-term change and relational leadership

If we want to change how leaders behave, we must engage how they *feel*—and how their brains react under pressure.

Six Neural Levers for Leadership Transformation

If we want leadership programs to truly transform behavior, not just awareness, we need to design programs for how the brain changes.

1. The Emotional Brain Reacts First

The amygdala responds to threat before the prefrontal cortex has time to assess. That means emotional reflexes often override logic.

For leadership to evolve, leaders must first notice their patterns. This starts with emotional self-awareness, a core adult learning principle that precedes self-regulation.

2. The Brain Can Rewire—But Not on Insight Alone

The brain's plasticity is real, but it requires:

- Repetition
- Emotional salience
- Time for integration

Adult learners need experiences that feel relevant and require them to apply new behaviors repeatedly in real situations. Content alone won't rewire behavior. Experience, feedback, and reflection will.

3. Identity Lives in the Brain

Leadership behaviors are entangled with identity. "This is just who I am," leaders often say. To shift behavior, programs must safely challenge this identity.

That means:

- Using narrative and story work

- Creating feedback-rich spaces

- Asking not just "What will I do?" but "Who am I becoming?"

These methods align with Jack Mezirow's transformative learning theory, which highlights perspective shifts as critical to adult development.

4. Reflection Is the Bridge to Integration

Reflection turns experience into growth. Journaling, peer dialogue, and post-experience debriefs deepen awareness and allow leaders to metabolize discomfort into insight.

Kolb's experiential learning cycle confirms this: reflection is a required step between experience and conceptual understanding.

5. Psychological Safety Unlocks Learning

Neuroscience shows that the brain interprets emotional risk as physical danger. Without safety, the learning brain shuts down. With it, learners become more curious, open, and resilient.

Programs must design for safety from the start, not assume it emerges. This includes:

- Norming vulnerability
- Training facilitators to model emotional transparency
- Encouraging inclusion and nonjudgmental feedback

Safety does not mean comfort. It means leaders can stretch without fear of shame.

6. Pattern Interrupt + Practice = Rewiring

Melissa didn't become more emotionally intelligent overnight. Her shift came from:

- Disrupting an old pattern (silence about personal struggle)
- Practicing a new response (vulnerability and listening)
- Receiving feedback in a safe space

Her new leadership loop became: **Feel → Pause → Choose → Lead**

It's that pause between stimulus and reaction, where transformation lives.

Research Spotlight: Emotion as Catalyst

In my research, the breakthrough moments weren't intellectual. They were emotional. Leaders remembered:

The first time they told their story

When they were given hard feedback, and stayed open

When they cried in a room and weren't judged

One leader shared, "The moment I got emotional wasn't weakness. That's when I got real. That's when the growth started."

Another said: "No model or framework we learned reached me like that moment did. I didn't just learn leadership—I became a leader."

These aren't sentimental anecdotes. They reflect what neuroscience and adult learning agree on: emotions anchor memory and motivate change.

What This Means for Leadership Development

T&D programs need to move beyond awareness and focus on building for transformation. That requires:

- **Interrupting emotional reflexes**: Surface old patterns and offer real-time opportunities to choose differently.

- **Creating safety to stretch**: Leaders must feel safe enough to take emotional risks.

- **Designing for the limbic brain**: Engage emotion, not just cognition.

- **Building repetition and reflection**: Cement learning through structured feedback, peer interaction, and integrated practice.

Melissa didn't transform because she understood emotional intelligence. She changed because she felt something, and then practiced doing something different.

Opportunity for Reflection

Think back to a leadership program you've delivered or attended:

- Did it invite emotional risk, or avoid it?

- Was there space for story, identity, or vulnerability?

- Where could you have created more opportunity for pause, discomfort, or deep connection?

Growth doesn't happen in the knowing. It occurs in the feeling and the doing.

Practice for T&D Leaders

Apply the six neural levers to your flagship leadership program:

1. **Audit for safety**: Do Facilitators Model Vulnerability? Is psychological safety actively maintained?

2. **Create stretch experiences**: Design one moment that gently prompts leaders to move beyond their default responses, such as storytelling, reflection on failure, or empathy interviews.

3. **Build in structured reflection**: Add 10 minutes of peer reflection to the end of each module. Provide prompts that move from the head to the heart.

4. **Prioritize emotional learning**: Introduce an early exercise where participants identify personal triggers and responses. Normalize discomfort.

5. **Use repeated practice**: Build skill drills into the program where participants try new behaviors across multiple sessions.

6. **Track integration, not attendance**: Use feedback journals, peer accountability, or 30-day post-program check-ins.

The most effective programs don't add content—they architect experience.

A Transition to What's Next

If change lives in the body—not just the brain—then our programs must evolve.

In the next chapter, we'll explore how to design emotionally intelligent learning journeys that embed change through immersion, stretch, and integration. You'll meet a leader whose transformation began not with strategy, but with silence.

Because the future doesn't need more polished performers, it requires leaders who are rewired, present, and real.

PART II

How to Design for
Transformational Growth

5

Designing Programs That Transform

The Shift That Changed Everything

Marcus had plateaued.

As a senior VP at a fast-scaling software company, he excelled at execution—hitting targets, managing high-performing teams, and earning recognition as a rising star. But something was missing. His leadership wasn't landing where it mattered most: with people.

Despite his results, Marcus struggled to retain senior talent. Feedback revealed a consistent pattern: overcontrolling, emotionally distant, quick to shut down dissent. He wasn't failing, but he wasn't fully leading. And his teams felt it.

He expected the usual surface-level workshop when he enrolled in a multi-week leadership program. What he found was different.

Gone were the lectures and frameworks. In their place: storytelling, feedback circles, emotional challenge, and honest reflection. In that space, Marcus met someone he hadn't seen in years—himself.

"I thought I needed new skills," he later said. "What I needed was a new way to be me."

This chapter explains how to develop leadership programs that foster this kind of internal shift—and why the future of leadership development hinges on emotional intelligence and identity change, rather than content mastery.

From Information to Transformation

Most leadership programs are built to deliver content. But emotional intelligence isn't downloaded—it's developed.

Leaders don't shift because someone told them to regulate their emotions. They change when they've had the emotional experience of losing control, and the supported space to understand why it happened and how to respond differently.

This distinction between learning *about* and learning *through* is the heart of transformative learning theory (Mezirow, 1991). Adults grow when experiences challenge their assumptions and prompt them to reexamine who they are.

Here are six design principles that help leadership programs move from information to transformation.

1. Build for Immersion, Not Interruption

You can't change how you lead between emails. Deep growth requires presence, not distraction.

Immersion doesn't just mean time away from the desk—it means emotional presence, disrupted routines, and a different kind of space where deeper parts of the self can emerge.

To design for immersion:

- **Use multi-week cohorts** with intentional pacing. Learning needs space to sink in, reflect, and integrate.

- **Incorporate off-site or retreat-style experiences.** Physical separation from work roles encourages psychological distance from old habits.

- **Design integration touchpoints** between sessions. Leaders need opportunities to apply, reflect on, and integrate their learning.

- **Use emotionally complex simulations.** These surface unconscious patterns accelerate behavioral experimentation.

"I didn't realize how checked-out I'd become," one executive shared. "Being immersed helped me hear myself again."

2. Prioritize Psychological Safety

It's simple, no safety, no growth.

Leaders won't take emotional risks—or engage with identity-level learning—if they feel judged. Safety is more than a ground rule; it's a feeling that must be cultivated every step of the way.

Strategies for cultivating safety:

- **Establish clear cohort agreements** around confidentiality and respect.

- **Model vulnerability early.** Facilitators who share authentically open the door for others.

- **Create opt-in paths** for deeper reflection exercises. Pressure undermines safety.

- **Dedicate processing space.** Not all insights come in the moment—leaders need time to process and integrate change.

"I only dropped the mask because I trusted the room. That trust changed everything."

As Amy Edmondson's research has shown, psychological safety enables experimentation, feedback, and ultimately, learning.

3. Design for Emotional Resonance

Adults don't change from facts—they change from moments.

Powerful learning experiences evoke emotional insight. They challenge leaders to confront what's unresolved, speak truths they've avoided, and feel things they've numbed.

Ways to create resonance:

- **Use storytelling as pedagogy.** Invite leaders to share defining leadership moments—not accomplishments, but trials.

- **Facilitate peer feedback circles.** Hearing how others experience you deepens reflection.

- **Include roleplays that mirror ethical tension.** Emotional discomfort unlocks internal shifts.

- **Build shared reflection into each session.** Ask: "What stirred something in you?"

"The moment I said it out loud—and wasn't judged—was the moment something shifted."

4. Engineer Stretch with Support

Growth happens when people reach beyond what's comfortable, but not so far that they panic.

Robert Kegan's concept of the "growth edge" applies here: real development lies just beyond the current capacity, in the zone where safety meets stretch.

Build this balance by:

- **Providing peer coaching before and after challenges.**

- **Framing emotional discomfort as part of the process: Normalize, rather than avoid, the challenge.**

- **Offering mid-session reflection points allows learners to process and then re-engage.**

- **Creating structured "return to center" moments after high-stakes exercises.**

"It was hard, but I wasn't alone in it—and that's what made me stay in the work."

Stretch without support leads to shutdown. With the right scaffolding, leaders grow.

5. Structure Reflection as Core Curriculum

Reflection isn't optional, it's where growth takes root.

Transformative learning relies on what Mezirow called "critical reflection": the ability to question assumptions, examine identity, and make meaning of experience.

Ways to embed reflection:

- **Use guided journaling every session.** Prompt internal connection, not just insight capture.
- **Create small-group debriefs.** Peer dialogue deepens perspective.
- **Introduce structured tools,** like the Learning Journal or Immunity to Change map.
- **Ask reflection-rich questions:**
  o What surprised you?
  o Where did you feel most reactive?
  o What old habit surfaced? What new possibility emerged?

"The sessions sparked insight. But the reflection—that's where it stuck."

6. Model the Behavior You're Teaching

Facilitators teach more by how they lead than what they say.

If you're developing emotional intelligence, your presence must embody it. This includes managing your own reactions, staying attuned to the group's energy, and leading with grounded authenticity.

Great facilitators:

- Are emotionally self-aware and regulated.
- Can sit with silence and emotion without rushing to fix.
- Adjust in real time based on group needs.
- Bring curiosity, not control.

"It wasn't just the curriculum—it was how the room was held. The facilitator was the work."

Facilitation isn't instruction. It's relational leadership in action.

Research Spotlight:
Design Immersive Stretch Experiences

In my research, the most transformational moments were immersive, emotionally intense, and socially supported.

Three examples:

- **Team-Based Filmmaking Challenge:** Leaders co-created a short film under pressure. Power dynamics emerged, and emotional intelligence, not positional authority, ultimately drove success. "I had to lead through vulnerability, not title."

- **Olympic Rowing Experience:** Executives rowed in crews with elite coaches. The only way forward was to trust, to have the right timing, and to let go of control. "I couldn't power through. I had to listen and sync."

- **Firefighting Simulation:** In a controlled but chaotic environment, leaders had to regulate under pressure. Emotional responses—fight, flight, freeze—became visible and coachable. "I saw myself panic. Then I chose differently."

These moments were effective because they were followed by structured and safe reflection.

What This Means for Leadership Development

We're not just designing programs—we're creating opportunities for personal and professional transformation.

To build emotionally intelligent leaders who can navigate AI-era complexity, our programs must:

- Interrupt reactive patterns.

- Evoke emotional truth.

- Combine challenge with care.

- Rehearse relational presence.

- Help leaders reclaim themselves.

The future of leadership isn't a toolkit—it's a rewiring.

Opportunity for Reflection

Think about a program you've led or experienced:

- Where did it evoke emotion, truth, or identity exploration?
- Where did the design support—or undercut—real behavior change?
- What design element could make it more emotionally impactful?

Practice for T&D Leaders

Add a Psychological Safety Diagnostic to your program kickoff.

Use a validated tool, such as the Edmondson Team Diagnostic Survey, as part of your intake or pre-work. Then:

1. **Analyze trends** in responses (e.g., low voice, fear of judgment).
2. **Tailor your facilitation strategy** to address vulnerabilities.
3. **Reassess safety** midway through the program to track progress.
4. **Use cohort insights** to refine program design for future runs.

This move transforms psychological safety from a value into a metric, making it something your program actively develops and can measure.

A Transition to What's Next

Transformation doesn't begin at the whiteboard—it starts with safety.

In the next chapter, we'll dive deeper into how psychological safety isn't a phase or an icebreaker. It's the very medium through which identity change becomes possible.

Because without safety, there's no risk. And without risk, there's no growth.

6

Safe Containers and the Deep Work of Identity Transformation

"This Is the First Time I've Felt Safe Enough to Change"

Erika had spent two decades leading high-performing teams in a results-driven, high-stakes culture. She was composed, capable, and—by all external measures—successful.

In her first peer feedback session during a multi-week immersive leadership program, she responded with polite detachment: "It's helpful. I appreciate the input."

Her coach didn't push.

A week later, during a small group storytelling session, another leader shared openly about a public failure and the fear of not being enough. The air shifted. Vulnerability cracked open the room.

Then Erika spoke.

"I've never said this before… I'm afraid if I ever stop performing, people will leave."

She cried. Not from weakness, but from release.

Later, she turned to her coach and said, "This is the first time I've felt safe enough to change."

That was the beginning, not of learning a new skill, but of becoming a different kind of leader.

Four Conditions for Identity-Level Growth

Transformational learning doesn't come from content alone. It arises when four essential conditions are present:

- **Emotional Safety** – Without it, leaders protect themselves with performance and pretense.

- **Meaningful Disruption** – A challenge that shakes old beliefs and opens a doorway to reflection.

- **Reflective Integration** – Time and space to make sense of what's emerging.

- **Relational Feedback** – Honest, caring feedback from peers who see both the leader and the human.

When these conditions converge, the shift isn't just behavioral—it's identity-level.

The Anatomy of a Transformational Container

In emotionally intelligent leadership development, the "container" is the curriculum.

It's not just the structure—it's the safety, norms, and presence that allow leaders to show up with truth.

"I didn't open up because the curriculum said I could," one executive said. "I opened up because the facilitator already had."

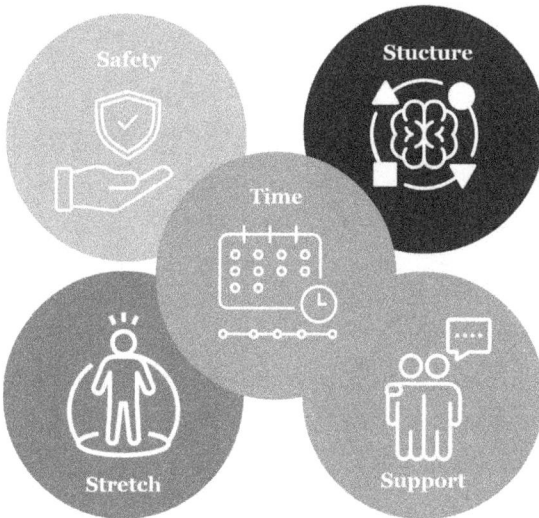

Key design elements of strong and effective containers for transformation:

Element	Purpose
Shared Agreements	Create boundaries for honesty and respect
Opt-In Vulnerability	Allow leaders to choose their depth—no forced sharing
Facilitator Modeling	Show vulnerability to invite it
Rituals for Opening/Closing	Signal the space is different— emotionally and psychologically
Peer Support	Normalize challenge, amplify connection

Psychological safety doesn't just happen—it must be deliberately built and actively held.

Stories as Gateways to Identity

Nothing disarms ego like a personal story. When leaders tell the truth about who they are and what shaped them, it opens the door to deeper transformation.

Neuroscience supports this claim: storytelling activates the limbic system, the emotional center of the brain, enhancing empathy, memory, and emotional salience (Zak, 2015).

In my research, one of the most transformational exercises was a storytelling-on-film challenge. Leaders recorded their own leadership journeys and watched them back with peers.

"It forced me to look in the mirror," one said. "I'd been hiding behind competence for years."

These narratives brought buried beliefs to light:

- "If I'm not in control, I'm failing."
- "If I show emotion, I'll lose credibility."
- "My value is my performance."

Once spoken aloud—and held with care—those stories began to shift.

Peer Feedback as a Mirror

When feedback is offered with care and clarity, it becomes a mirror—reflecting not just behavior, but impact.

One executive shared: "Hearing my impact from a peer changed me, not because they were harsh, but because I knew they cared enough to be honest."

In a strong container, leaders learn to:

- Receive input without defensiveness
- Separate intention from impact
- Test new behaviors in real time

When you set the conditions, the growth zone emerges:

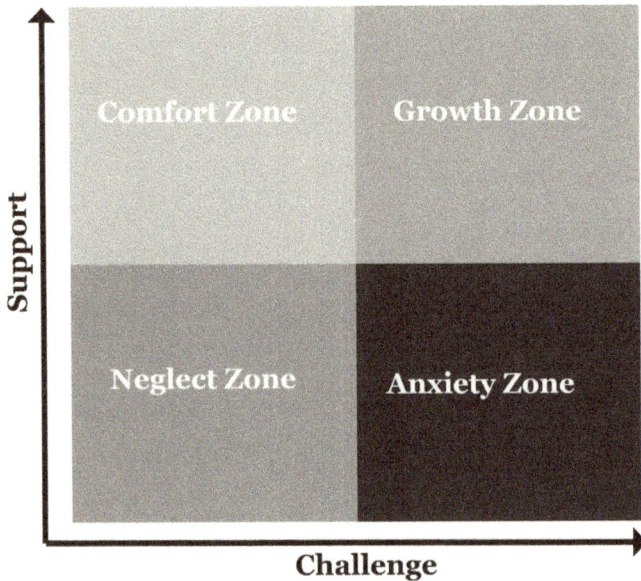

When participants feel safe and supported, they can take on challenges that push them well outside of their comfort zone.

This is a "practice space" for identity, not just behavior. Leaders begin to hear themselves through others' eyes and grow into the person they're becoming.

Facilitators as Architects of Emotion Experiences

Facilitators aren't just teaching content. They are modeling the very presence, attunement, and emotional courage they hope to draw out.

The best facilitators:

- Stay calm when the group isn't
- Invite emotion, but don't perform it
- Model humility, not perfection
- Respond without rushing to solve

"It wasn't the slide deck," one participant said. "It was how the facilitator held the room. That changed everything."

A strong facilitator makes emotional complexity feel navigable, not dangerous.

The Arc of Identity Transformation

True transformation tends to follow a predictable arc:

1. **Disruption** – A moment that breaks old mental models

2. **Reflection** – Internal inquiry, meaning-making, emotional integration

3. **Dialogue** – Peer support that affirms and stretches insight

4. **Reintegration** – A new story, a new stance, a shift in how the leader shows up

This arc is rooted in adult learning theory, which posits that adults grow not through instruction but through meaning-making in response to challenges (Mezirow, 1997).

Reintegration: New self-understanding
applied to real work/life

Support: Coaching, peer
dialogue, or community-based
integration

Reflection: Deep questioning
and journaling about identity
or impact

Disruption: A moment
that unsettles assumptions
(e.g., failure, feedback)

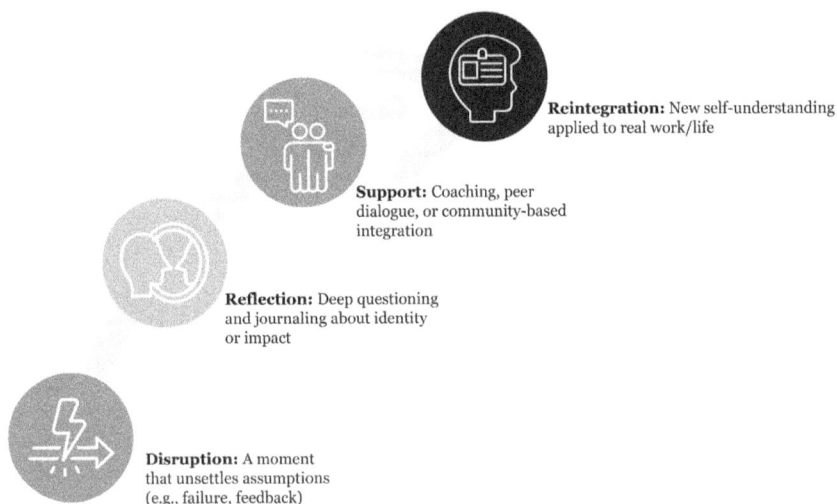

Designing for identity-level growth means structuring learning experiences around this arc, rather than just delivering content.

Designing for Deep Learning

To build programs that foster identity-level transformation, T&D teams must:

- **Put the container before the curriculum** – Safety is the soil where truth can take root.

- **Start with story, not slides** – Connection creates capacity.

- **Value practice over performance** – Leaders must try new behaviors before perfecting them.

- **Prioritize presence over polish** – Leaders need to feel safe showing up imperfectly.

Specific tactics include:

- Opening with authentic storytelling exercises

- Incorporating guided journaling and group debriefs

- Using facilitated peer feedback that centers care and clarity

- Designing rituals that signal "this space is different"

When these elements are integrated, change becomes more than possible—it becomes probable.

What This Means for Leadership Development

Traditional programs often stop at behavior. But emotionally intelligent leadership takes root at the level of identity.

To meet this challenge, T&D must:

- Design experiences that foster emotional safety and truth-telling

- Use stories and peer feedback to surface hidden beliefs

- Support leaders through the discomfort of change, not avoid it

This isn't soft. It's foundational.

If we want leaders who can remain grounded during disruption, we must provide them with a space to be honest, connected, and whole.

Opportunity for Reflection

Think about a leadership program you've created, led, or joined:

- Where did it create real emotional safety?

- When did you—or others—tell a deeper truth?

- How might a stronger container have enabled more transformation?

Practice for T&D Leaders

Run a container audit on your most critical leadership programs. Ask:

- Do we open with vulnerability—or with logistics?

- Do facilitators model emotional intelligence, or merely discuss it?

- Are there structured opportunities for story, feedback, and reflection?

Then pilot one change: add a personal storytelling exercise in week one, facilitated by someone who can model depth without oversharing. Track the shift in group tone and trust.

Conclusion: Belonging Is the Threshold

Transformation begins when leaders stop performing and start becoming. But they can't get there alone. Before leaders can guide others through change, they must feel safe enough to face their own. Before they can build a sense of belonging for others, they must experience it for themselves. Belonging is the threshold. Safety is the door. Transformation is what waits on the other side.

A Transition to What's Next

In the next chapter, we explore how peer dynamics and cohort-based learning amplify emotional intelligence—why connection isn't just support, but a multiplier for insight, growth, and sustainable change.

7

The Power of Peer Dynamics and Cohort-Based Learning

"I Couldn't Hide. And That Was the Gift."

Marcus had always seen himself as a composed, results-driven leader. He ran large business units with precision, kept emotions at bay, and believed vulnerability belonged at home, not at work.

Then came the immersive leadership program.

In the early weeks, Marcus kept his distance. During peer check-ins, he offered polished answers, steering clear of emotional depth. He didn't want to appear weak.

But in week three, something shifted. A fellow executive shared a story about failing to support a team member during a mental health crisis. No one flinched. The room held steady. Everyone leaned in.

That moment cracked something open for Marcus.

By week five, he was sharing stories about his father's emotional distance—and how it shaped his discomfort with empathy. His peers didn't judge. They embraced him.

"That cohort held up a mirror I'd avoided for years," he reflected. "I couldn't hide. And that was the gift."

Marcus didn't just shift his leadership style. He rewrote the internal narrative that had kept him guarded for years. And that shift came not through content, but through connection.

Why Peer Dynamics Matter in Leadership Development

Emotional intelligence is forged in relationships, not in isolation. You can't learn to lead with empathy, regulate emotion, or build trust by reading a book, not even this one.

Leaders grow through:

- **Real-time feedback** on blind spots
- **New perspectives** that challenge assumptions
- **Emotional modeling** by others
- **Shared vulnerability** and mutual accountability

These aren't optional. They're the engine of transformation.

As one executive put it: "The curriculum was solid. But it was my peers who showed me the parts of myself I'd been avoiding."

Peer learning unlocks three critical capacities: self-awareness, emotional resilience, and the courage to change.

The Social Mirror: Seeing Ourselves Through Others

Facilitators can offer guidance. Peers reflect impact.

In high-trust cohorts, leaders receive:

- Unfiltered reactions to their behavior

- Honest but caring reflections

- Opportunities to try new behaviors and get feedback in real time

One leader recalled: "I didn't realize how often I interrupted until a peer gently pointed it out. That changed how I listen."

These micro-moments recalibrate leadership identity. Leaders begin to see not just who they are, but who they're becoming.

Trust Takes Time: The Case for Cohort Continuity

Psychological safety isn't built in a day. It emerges through:

- Repeated interactions

- Emotional disclosure

- Shared norms

- Consistency over time

Adult learning theory tells us that emotional safety is a prerequisite for exploration and growth (Kolb, Mezirow, Knowles). When participants feel seen and accepted, they're more likely to take emotional risks.

Cohorts designed for continuity become:

- **Containers** for emotional risk

- **Mirrors** for self-reflection

- **Communities** of shared belonging

In this environment, performance drops away and presence emerges.

Research Spotlight: Belonging and Identity Shifts

In my research, participants rarely recalled frameworks first—they remembered the cohort. "It wasn't the content. It was the connection."

Repeatedly, executives described how peer environments helped dismantle old internal scripts:

- *"I have to hold it all together."*

- *"If I'm vulnerable, I'll lose credibility."*

- *"Everyone else has it figured out."*

These limiting beliefs weren't challenged with logic. They were softened through presence.

Executives described firsts:

- Crying in front of colleagues

- Admitting fears about their leadership

- Receiving support without needing to earn it

Belonging was the catalyst. "The cohort gave me permission to lead differently. Not just better—but more honestly."

Peer Dialogue as Emotional Practice Ground

You can't practice emotional intelligence in isolation. It's a social muscle.

Cohorts provide a lab where leaders rehearse:

- Listening deeply—especially under stress

- Setting boundaries with empathy

- Engaging in conflict without withdrawal

- Naming emotion and holding space for others

This is the human side of leadership. And it must be practiced in the company of humans, not in solitude.

"That circle kept me honest," one executive said. "I showed up differently because they cared enough to expect more."

These conversations are messy. They're also where the real growth happens.

Here are some examples of peer-based activities and observed benefits from effective leadership development programs in my research:

Peer Interaction Type	EI Competencies Practiced	Observed Benefits
Storytelling Circles	Empathy, Self-awareness, Vulnerability	Increased trust and depth of connection within the cohort
Feedback Exchanges	Self-regulation, Social skill, Openness to feedback	More honest conversations and reduced defensiveness
Group Conflict Resolution	Emotional regulation, Conflict management, Trust-building	Improved ability to address tension constructively
Case Debrief Dialogues	Reflection, Perspective-taking, Active listening	Greater self-awareness and behavior tracking
Peer Accountability Moments	Personal responsibility, Growth mindset, Integrity	Stronger follow-through on behavior change

Designing for Constructive Peer Accountability

When done well, peer dynamics don't just comfort. They stretch.

In high-performing cohorts, peers:

- Call out misalignments between values and actions

- Hold each other to the work, without shame

- Model what it means to give and receive honest feedback

"They didn't let me hide—and that changed everything," one leader shared.

This kind of accountability builds trust, not tension. It invites integrity.

What This Means for Leadership Development

To embed emotional intelligence in your programs:

- **Design for cohort continuity and safety.** Trust requires time.

- **Facilitate peer dialogue as emotional rehearsal.** It's not fluff—it's the work.

- **Treat belonging as a design principle, not a byproduct.** It's the container where identity change happens.

No slide deck can match the power of being seen, challenged, and supported by peers walking the same road.

Opportunity for Reflection

If you're a T&D leader or program designer:

- Where does your current design create space for authentic peer connection?

- When do participants feel seen, and when might they be performing?

- What might happen if your next cohort stayed together longer and went deeper?

Practice for T&D Leaders

Pilot a Peer Coaching Circle: In your next leadership program:

1. Form peer triads or quartets for the full duration.

2. Provide loose structure, rotating facilitators, shared agreements, and check-in prompts.

3. Equip participants with basic coaching tools (e.g., active listening, reflecting back, asking open-ended questions).

4. Encourage discussion of real-time leadership challenges—not just concepts.

5. Close with reflection: "What did you notice about yourself in this conversation?"

These circles become micro-ecosystems of growth—spaces where leaders practice vulnerability, curiosity, and accountability.

Conclusion: Designing for Human Connection

Leadership development is often framed as an individual pursuit. But emotional intelligence is relational.

If we want leaders who are more:

- Empathetic
- Self-aware
- Resilient

We must:

- Design for sustained peer interaction

- Normalize emotional risk and feedback

- Build containers of belonging—not just curriculum

Because no model can teach what it means to be fully seen and still supported, that's the work of a cohort. That's the beginning of transformation.

A Transition to What's Next

In the next chapter, we'll explore one of the most underestimated drivers of transformation: time. We'll look at why behavior change doesn't just need intensity—it requires consistency because change takes space, not speed.

8

The Immersive Advantage & Why Duration Matters

Wk1 • • • • • • • • • • • • • • • • • • ▶ Wk8

The Experience That Couldn't Be Rushed

Sanjay had completed dozens of leadership trainings across his 25-year career. Most were efficient, packed into a day or two of slides and frameworks, followed by polite applause, and a swift return to the daily grind.

Then came the 8-week immersive leadership program.

He expected another exercise in corporate compliance. Instead, it began with something disarming: a request to tell his leadership story—not his résumé, but the moments that shaped him. What had stretched him? What still lived behind the mask he wore?

By week four, Sanjay's default defenses—control, certainty, and performance—began to loosen. His peers didn't just hear his words; they noticed his patterns.

By week seven, he was experimenting with a new kind of leadership: pausing instead of reacting, listening instead of fixing, revealing instead of hiding. "I've never been this clear about how I lead—or why it matters that I do it differently."

Sanjay didn't just finish a program. He crossed a threshold. And that shift was possible only because the program gave him the one thing most leadership development doesn't: time.

Why Duration Matters

T&D professionals often hear, "Our leaders don't have time." But deep learning—the kind that rewires emotional habits and reshapes identity—doesn't happen in a single afternoon. You can't microwave transformation. It takes more than exposure to ideas. It takes immersion, repetition, and space for reflection.

Short-format programs can spark awareness, offer tools, or shift a mindset. But sustainable change requires continuity. It requires a structure that honors how adults learn and change over time, in community, through application.

This principle is grounded in key tenets of adult learning theory:

- **Andragogy** (Knowles): Adults are self-directed learners who bring lived experience into the learning process. They need time and context to integrate new concepts.

- **Transformative Learning** (Mezirow): Critical reflection and identity shifts occur when learners engage over time with disorienting dilemmas in psychologically safe environments.

- **Experiential Learning** (Kolb): Learning cycles of experience, reflection, conceptualization, and experimentation require duration and depth to fully unfold.

What Time Makes Possible

Multi-week programs create what leaders rarely experience in fast-paced work environments: space to evolve. That space allows for four transformational processes to take root:

- **Deep Emotional Engagement** – Leaders can't process vulnerability or challenge in a 60-minute block. They need time to metabolize emotions and revisit patterns with new insight.

- **Behavioral Rehearsal** – Emotional intelligence is a skill, not a trait. Leaders need chances to try, fail, recalibrate, and try again—in real scenarios, across multiple sessions.

- **Cohort-Based Trust** – Trust doesn't arrive on demand. It forms through repeated interaction, shared vulnerability, and the passage of time. By week four, posturing fades. Real relationships emerge.

- **Identity Work** – The most profound shifts don't change what leaders do—they change how they see themselves. That kind of work can't be rushed.

"Day one was about showing up. The days that followed were about showing up as me."

Six Reasons Immersion Drives Transformation

1. **Immersion Interrupts the Default Loop** – Most leadership behavior runs on autopilot. Extended immersion interrupts that loop and creates a space to choose different responses. "Previous trainings gave me better tools. This gave me a new lens."

2. **Trust Takes Time** – Psychological safety isn't a checkbox—it's an emotional state. Leaders need space to let their guard down. "It took three sessions for me to stop pretending. Only then could I start growing."

3. **Repetition Builds Muscle** – You can't practice emotional regulation or boundary-setting once and expect mastery. Repetition enables rewiring. It reinforces new behavior through experience.

4. **Integration Requires Space** – Insight without integration fades. Breaks between sessions give leaders time to apply concepts, reflect, and return with questions. This spacing effect improves retention and transformation.

5. **Cohort Continuity Amplifies Growth** – A stable cohort provides consistent feedback, challenge, and a sense of belonging. It becomes both mirror and container. "My cohort saw me fall apart—and still held me. That made it safe to rebuild differently."

6. **Emotional Sequencing Shapes the Arc** – The best programs don't just last, they flow. They follow an emotional arc that mirrors how adults actually learn and change:

   o **Weeks 1–2:** Psychological safety and orientation

   o **Weeks 3–4:** Disruption, challenge, and initial reflection

   o **Weeks 5–7:** Identity exploration and emotional risk

   o **Weeks 8–10:** Integration, practice, and forward planning

This arc aligns with how transformative learning unfolds: not through content delivery, but through emotional engagement and reflection.

Research Spotlight: Transformation Takes Time

In my research, participants in immersive executive programs consistently reported that time was not a luxury—it was the precondition for growth.

Key findings:

- **Trust took time**: "The real breakthrough didn't happen in the room. It happened between sessions."

- **Reflection needed space**: "At first, I didn't get it. Then, two weeks later, something landed—and I saw myself differently."

- **Behavior change was iterative**: Reactions surfaced, habits were tested, and leaders learned by doing, over and over again.

- **Identity shifts required emotional repetition**: Participants needed multiple safe exposures to feedback and vulnerability to begin internal transformation.

A comparative analysis of short-form vs. immersive programs showed stark contrasts:

Format	Observed Outcome
Short-form workshops	Increased awareness, low retention of EI behaviors
Immersive programs	Sustained behavior change, identity-level transformation, emotional agility under pressure

"Quick-hit trainings gave me content. This gave me clarity—and change."

What This Means for Leadership Development

If you're designing programs to foster emotionally intelligent leaders, here's what matters:

- **Design for duration**: Consider multi-week formats. Even four-week arcs create more space for identity work than one-day events.

- **Sequence for emotional resonance**: Begin with safety, then invite stretch. Support reflection and closure at the end.

- **Embed reflective and relational practices**: Rehearsal, journaling, peer feedback—these practices support long-term change.

- **Honor the learner's timeline**: Not everyone changes at the same pace. Design flexibly to meet learners where they are.

This is not indulgence. It's infrastructure for transformation.

Opportunity for Reflection

If you're a T&D leader or facilitator:

- Where in your programs is there time for emotional digestion, not just idea exposure?

- Do you provide participants with multiple opportunities to practice, reflect, and recalibrate?

- Are you sequencing experiences to follow the arc of emotional readiness and identity evolution?

Practice for T&D Leaders

Design leadership development programs with emotional arcs in mind. Break your leadership program into distinct phases:

1. **Welcome + Emotional Safety:**

   o Begin with storytelling, agreements, and lightly facilitated connection.

   o Use tools like psychological safety surveys to establish group baselines (Edmondson, 2019).

2. **Challenge + Reflection:**

   o Introduce simulations, case tensions, or identity exercises around Week 3–4.

   o Include structured debriefs and journaling prompts (e.g., "What's being challenged in me right now?").

3. **Experimentation + Rehearsal:**

   o Facilitate peer coaching or live scenario testing across Weeks 5–7.

   o Offer tools like emotional scripts, centering techniques, and boundary practice.

4. **Integration + Closure:**

   o Conclude with identity mapping, leadership commitment letters, or a reflective roundtable.

   o Give space for individual action planning and peer feedback loops.

This arc supports not just cognitive insight, but emotional and behavioral integration.

Conclusion: Depth Over Doses

Sanjay's transformation wasn't a flash of brilliance. It was a slow burn. A series of small openings led to a significant shift.

What made the difference?

- Immersion interrupted his patterns.

- Time gave him space to reflect.

- Repetition let him practice.

- Trust turned a group into a container.

- Emotional sequencing guided his arc.

In an era obsessed with speed, leadership development must choose depth.

Immersion isn't a luxury. It's how real change happens.

A Transition to What's Next

The final session isn't the end. In many ways, it's the beginning.

In the next chapter, we explore how to sustain momentum after the program ends through coaching, peer support, and structures that help leaders live their insight long after the room clears.

Because even the most powerful moment fades...unless someone reminds you and helps you integrate the lessons.

9

Coaching, Dialogue, and Sustaining the Transformation

"The Program Changed Me. The Coaching Helped Me Live It."

Ryan walked out of his immersive leadership program with a renewed sense of purpose. He was more grounded, more emotionally available, and more connected to his team. But within weeks, the pressure of deadlines and deliverables returned. Stress crept back in. Old habits—controlling, fixing, reacting—took hold.

What brought him back wasn't a workbook or slide deck. It was a conversation.

During a coaching session, his coach gently reminded him of a powerful moment from the program—when Ryan had stood before his peers and named his fear of failure. That memory re-centered him. Together, they rehearsed how to navigate an upcoming high-stakes meeting by leading with empathy rather than anxiety.

"The coaching didn't give me new insight," Ryan reflected. "It reminded me how to live what I already knew."

That is the power of continuity. Coaching and peer dialogue don't just reinforce learning, they extend transformation into the moments that matter most.

The Cycle of Transformational Coaching

Coaching grounded in emotional intelligence isn't about offering answers. It's about guiding leaders back to themselves. At its best, coaching creates a structured space where adult learners reflect, question, and grow, building the muscle of self-awareness and self-regulation over time.

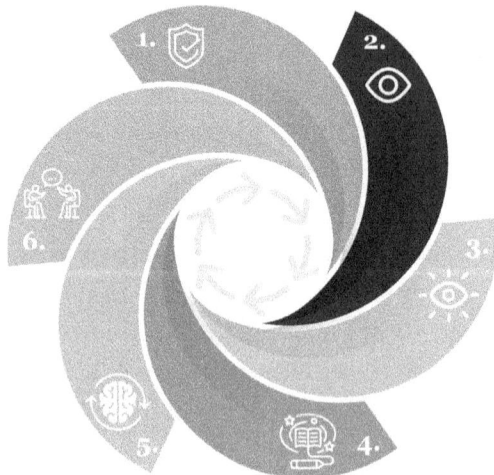

Here's how that cycle often unfolds:

1. Initiate the Container

Coaches create a space of psychological safety. Confidentiality, presence, and emotional clarity set the tone. This step aligns with adult learning theory, which suggests that readiness to learn is influenced by emotional security.

2. Reveal the Pattern

Through deep listening and open-ended questions, coaches help leaders surface recurring emotional triggers, reactive patterns, and internal narratives that drive behavior.

3. Deepen the Insight

Together, they explore the story underneath the response. What fear or belief is driving the action? What values are at stake?

4. Rehearse New Responses

The coaching session becomes a lab. Leaders experiment with new ways of showing up—pausing before reacting, asking instead of assuming, listening instead of fixing.

5. Reintegrate with Intention

Insights are applied in real-life leadership moments. The leader reflects on what worked, what didn't, and how to adjust.

6. Sustain Through Practice

Growth isn't linear. Reflection, feedback, and recommitment become a rhythm.

This is not performance coaching. It's identity-based coaching. It strengthens the leader from the inside out.

"My coach didn't tell me what to do," one executive shared. "They helped me remember who I wanted to be."

Coaching as Infrastructure, Not an Add-On

In adult learning, reflection and application are as important as exposure to content. Coaching extends both. It provides:

- A **pause** from reactivity to reflect with intention
- A **container** for processing emotional insight
- A **mirror** for ongoing self-awareness
- A **structure** for applying new behaviors with accountability

Unlike advising, coaching doesn't provide a solution. It develops. And when paired with emotionally intelligent leadership training, it anchors the transformation leaders begin in the room.

When Insight Fades, Coaching Anchors It

The most powerful moments in leadership programs are often emotionally charged. But emotions fade. Without reinforcement, even the most profound insights can be lost to:

- Information overload

- Workplace urgency

- Leadership isolation

- Default behavioral patterns

Coaching keeps the learning alive—long enough for it to become embodied.

"I knew who I wanted to be in the program," Ryan said. "Coaching helped me keep becoming that person after it ended."

Designing for Continuity

Programs often stop at delivery. The best ones plan for what comes next.

To support identity-level change, include structures that extend beyond the final session:

1:1 Executive Coaching

Tailored support for high-stakes moments, emotional regulation, and practicing new responses under pressure.

Peer Coaching Circles

Facilitated small groups for regular check-ins, accountability, and community. These reinforce belonging and normalize vulnerability.

Dialogue-Based Integration Sessions

Monthly or quarterly sessions that re-engage participants in shared reflection and structured practice. Think of them as booster shots for emotional intelligence.

These aren't perks, they're performance infrastructure.

Sustaining Emotional Intelligence in Practice

Emotional intelligence, like fitness, isn't a one-time event. It requires deliberate practice, reflection, and reinforcement.

Ongoing coaching helps leaders:

- **Normalize emotional discomfort** instead of avoiding it

- **Practice presence and empathy** under stress

- **Name emotions** instead of acting from them

- **Recommit to values** in difficult moments

- **Sustain identity-level growth** when pressure mounts

"The program opened the door," one participant said. "Coaching helped me walk through it—and keep walking."

Research Spotlight: Continuity Drives Retention

In my research, leaders who engaged in structured follow-up, coaching, peer dialogue, or reflection sessions reported:

- Higher retention of emotional intelligence language

- More consistent application of behaviors under stress

- Greater relational trust with teams

- Increased resilience in complexity

One executive summed it up: "In the program, I woke up. In coaching, I stayed awake."

What This Means for T&D

To create leadership programs that don't just inform but transform, T&D professionals must:

- Treat coaching as part of the core learning architecture, not a bolt-on

- Build peer dialogue into the design from the start

- Create post-program structures for reinforcement and reflection

- Normalize continuous emotional development, not just performance improvement

Transformation is not a single event. It's a pattern of remembering, reflecting, and recommitting.

Opportunity for Reflection

If you're a T&D leader or program designer, ask yourself:

- Where does the program end—and does it have to?

- How do you structure support for identity-level change after the "event"?

- What are your leaders practicing—or forgetting—once they leave your learning environment?

Practice for T&D Leaders

Design a post-program sustainment plan with built-in coaching rhythms. Here's a practical approach:

- **At 30 days**: Schedule a 1:1 or group coaching session focused on identity reflection—What patterns are returning? What values need reinforcement?

- **At 60 days**: Facilitate a dialogue-based peer session focused on live challenges and mutual support. Share failures as well as wins.

- **At 90 days**: Conduct a structured reflection workshop that links program insights to current leadership behaviors. Invite recommitment, not just review.

Track participation. Assess impact. Evolve based on feedback.

Conclusion: Where Growth Takes Root

Insight is the spark. Integration is the work.

Programs spark the flame, but coaching keeps it lit. It helps leaders:

- Remember who they want to be
- Practice emotionally intelligent habits under pressure
- Reconnect to their values in real time

Without continuity, growth stalls. With it, transformation becomes sustainable.

A Transition to What's Next

Coaching sustains personal change. But to scale emotionally intelligent leadership, we need to embed it across the organization.

In the next chapter, we explore how to embed emotional intelligence into the fabric of organizational life through rituals, systems, and culture. Because when transformation lives in the many, it becomes sustainable.

PART III

Scaling Emotional Intelligence
Across Systems

10

Embedding Emotional Intelligence into Organizational DNA

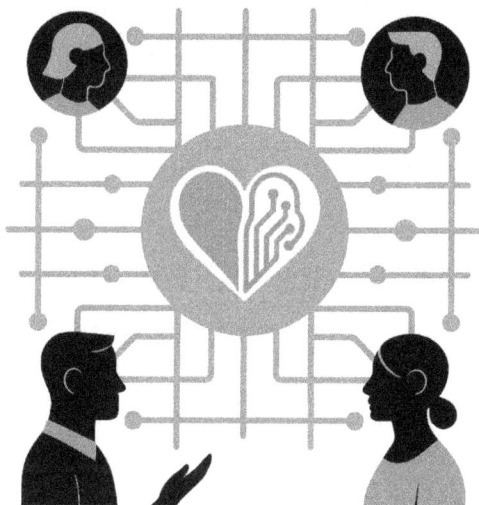

"You Can Feel It in the Culture."

When Anika stepped into the COO role at a midsize tech company, she noticed it immediately: decisions were fast, but reactions were faster.

Managers avoided difficult conversations. Meetings were efficient, but emotionally vacant. Employee engagement scores were falling, despite compensation increases and new perks.

"We had brilliant people," Anika reflected. "But no emotional bandwidth. Everyone was trying to win alone."

So she did something unconventional. She didn't launch a leadership workshop or host a retreat. She introduced a company-wide emotionally intelligent leadership initiative, starting with herself, but extending to every layer of the business. HR embedded it into onboarding. Mid-level managers got trained. Executive coaching became the norm, not the exception.

A year later, the company's engagement scores had jumped 26%. Voluntary attrition had dropped by half. And perhaps most telling of all, Anika started hearing something she had never heard in her first 90 days: "This place feels different."

Not because the mission changed. Because the emotional tone did.

When Emotional Intelligence Becomes Culture

Emotional intelligence is often seen as an individual strength—something you either possess or don't. But in practice, it works best when it's collective. When empathy, self-awareness, and emotional regulation are practiced across teams and supported by systems, they evolve into a cultural foundation.

In emotionally intelligent organizations:

- **Trust** is built deliberately, not assumed.
- **Feedback** is developmental, not punitive.
- **Empathy** is strategic, not sentimental.
- **Inclusion** is real, not just branded.

None of this happens by accident. These cultures are intentionally designed and sustained.

The Pyramid of Sustainable EI

Shifting from isolated learning events to a culture rooted in emotional intelligence requires the systemic alignment of five key elements.

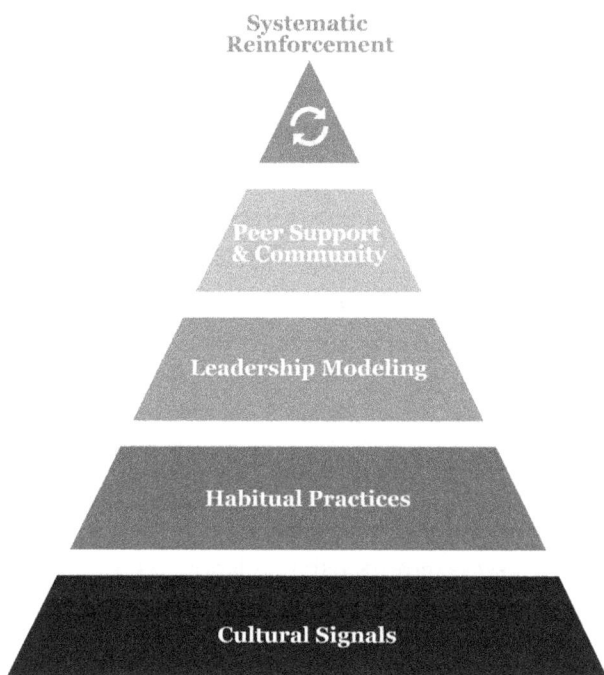

The following five layers support that shift:

1. **Cultural Signals** – Stories, symbols, and rituals that reflect what's truly valued, not just what's said.

2. **Habitual Practices** – Day-to-day behaviors like empathy-based feedback, active listening, and emotional check-ins.

3. **Leadership Modeling** – Leaders who model presence, composure, and care set the tone for everyone else.

4. **Peer Accountability** – Teams that challenge, support, and reinforce one another's growth amplify the culture.

5. **Systemic Reinforcement** – Policies, performance reviews, and reward systems that align with emotionally intelligent values.

When all five layers are aligned, emotionally intelligent leadership becomes part of "how we do things around here."

Operationalizing Emotional Intelligence

To embed EI at scale, organizations must operationalize it across the talent lifecycle, beyond leadership development alone. This means building it into how people are hired, developed, evaluated, and rewarded—not as an add-on, but as a core competency required to thrive in today's workplace.

Concrete strategies include:

- **Behavioral Interviewing for EI** – Structure interview questions to assess emotional regulation, empathy, and conflict navigation. Ask candidates to describe times they gave or received difficult feedback, how they responded to interpersonal tension, or how they managed emotional stress during change.

- **Onboarding for Belonging** – Reframe early employee experiences to establish psychological safety and emotional clarity. Instead of information dumps, begin with values-based storytelling, inclusive rituals, and intentional introductions that help new hires feel seen.

- **Performance Reviews Aligned to EI** – Incorporate relational and emotional competencies into evaluation rubrics, such as how a leader contributes to psychological safety, handles conflict, or nurtures team dynamics. Use 360° feedback to capture the full picture.

- **Rewards & Recognition Systems** – Recognize not just outcomes but how results are achieved. Acknowledge behaviors that model empathy, active listening, or vulnerability in service of growth. Incentivize leaders who create environments where others thrive.

- **Partnering Across the Enterprise** – Talent and development leaders should collaborate with HR, DEI, talent acquisition, and business unit heads to integrate EI into the enterprise's systems. For example:

  o Partner with HR to audit promotion and evaluation processes for alignment with emotionally intelligent leadership behaviors.

  o Collaborate with DEI leaders to ensure emotional literacy supports inclusion efforts.

  o Support product and tech teams by offering tools to help managers navigate the moral and ethical dilemmas and organizational dynamics of building and deploying AI and automation.

When these practices are embedded into organizational infrastructure, emotional intelligence becomes measurable, actionable, and scalable.

Cascading Culture, Not Just Command

Culture is not shaped by executive decree—everyday behaviors at every level of leadership shape it. To embed EI across the organization, leadership development must cascade intentionally from the top down and from the inside out.

Here's how to do it:

- **Start with Leadership Alignment** – Begin with the senior-most leaders. Facilitate immersive learning experiences that deepen self-awareness, model vulnerability, and create shared language around emotionally intelligent leadership. Senior leaders must lead the way, not just to "sponsor" change, but to embody it.

- **Build Manager Enablement Tracks** – Equip mid-level leaders with tools to model EI in day-to-day operations. This includes:

  o Conversation frameworks for emotionally complex dialogues

  o Practical tools for regulating stress in fast-paced settings

  o Opportunities for peer coaching and scenario-based learning

- **Create Cultural Multiplier Roles** – Identify culture carriers—respected employees at all levels who naturally lead with emotional intelligence. Engage them in co-creating rituals, leading feedback loops, or mentoring peers. These multipliers often hold more cultural influence than positional leaders.

- **Use T&D as a Cultural Architect** – As a T&D leader, your role is not just to deliver programs—it's to design the conditions for culture to cascade. This includes curating leadership models, shaping shared language, and reinforcing behaviors in partnership with cross-functional leaders.

When every level of leadership is aligned and equipped to lead with emotional intelligence, cultural change becomes exponential, not just linear.

Rituals That Reinforce Culture

Rituals are the heartbeat of emotionally intelligent organizations. They make values visible and transform intent into behavior. However, they must be intentional, repeatable, and aligned with the emotional tone you want to establish.

Add these practical rituals across the employee experience:

- **Weekly "Red, Yellow, Green" Check-ins** – Begin team meetings with a quick emotional status update: red (overwhelmed), yellow (stretched), or green (steady). No fixing—just awareness. This cultivates psychological safety and gives leaders insight into team well-being.

- **"Fail Forward" Story Circles** – Monthly team forums where leaders and employees share missteps, what they learned, and how they grew. These normalize vulnerability and encourage a growth mindset.

- **Post-Mortems with an EI Lens** – After projects or launches, reflect not just on results but on emotional experience: How did the team navigate pressure? Where did emotional friction emerge? What would we do differently next time?

- **Manager Listening Hours** – Allocate dedicated time for managers to hold unstructured sessions for emotional dialogue, particularly during periods of organizational change, restructuring, or AI deployment. These are not strategy meetings—they're presence practices.

- **Recognition of EI Behaviors** – Celebrate moments of courage, compassion, and authentic connection. Make "how" as visible as "what." This signals to the organization that emotional intelligence matters at every level.

By building these rituals into team rhythms, you foster environments where EI is felt, practiced, and spread organically.

Becoming the New Learning Organization

Peter Senge's vision of a learning organization—one that continually expands its capacity to grow and adapt—has never been more relevant. In the age of AI and exponential change, emotionally intelligent learning organizations hold a strategic edge. But the principles must be updated for today's context.

To become a modern learning organization infused with emotional intelligence, T&D must lead the integration across:

People

- Equip employees to process uncertainty and engage with change, emotionally and cognitively.

- Create cross-functional learning pods that prioritize empathy, inquiry, and reflection over pure efficiency.

- Encourage managers to coach rather than direct, fostering adaptive thinking and emotional resilience.

Processes

- Design learning pathways that reflect real emotional arcs of growth: safety, challenge, reflection, integration.

- Move away from one-size-fits-all training to flexible, human-centered development ecosystems.

- Embed learning into workflows, not just classrooms, so that leaders practice EI in the flow of work.

Technology

- Utilize AI tools to personalize learning, but strike a balance between automation and human connection. For example:

  o Pair AI-generated skill recommendations with peer coaching opportunities.

  o Utilize sentiment analysis to monitor emotional well-being and identify areas that require intervention.

  o Offer reflective journaling prompts and self-coaching nudges via internal platforms.

- Design learning platforms that prioritize *emotional user experience*, not just UI/UX. This means:

  o Reducing cognitive load

  o Promoting psychological safety in social learning forums

  o Encouraging emotionally resonant content

When emotional intelligence is baked into the way your organization learns—across people, process, and tech—you don't just teach EI. You live it.

Research Spotlight: Culture + EI = Outcomes

In my research, organizations that successfully embedded EI into their systems and culture consistently outperformed peers in key areas:

- **Engagement:** Sustained increases in employee engagement (+20% average over 12 months)

- **Retention:** Voluntary turnover dropped by 15–30% in high-EI environments

- **Psychological Safety:** Teams reported feeling safer to take risks and speak up

- **Performance Under Pressure:** EI-enabled teams handled crises with more cohesion and less burnout

One executive put it this way: "I used to think EI was about being nice. Now I know—it's about being a better, more effective human—and building a better place to work."

What This Means for Leadership Development

For T&D professionals, this insight is pivotal:

You can't scale transformation by developing individuals alone. You have to design the system they return to.

This means shifting:

- From **one-off events** to **ongoing ecosystems**
- From **training programs** to **cultural alignment**
- From **momentary growth** to **sustained transformation**

EI becomes a lever for performance, not value-added training.

Opportunity for Reflection

Ask yourself:

- Where does emotional intelligence live in your organization? Is it centralized or distributed?

- What rituals reinforce it—or quietly erode it?

- How do your performance and promotion systems support emotionally intelligent leadership?

Practice for T&D Leaders

Conduct a cross-functional EI culture audit. Here's how:

1. **Assess rituals** – Review key meetings, onboarding, and feedback systems. Where is EI visible? Where is it missing?

2. **Evaluate systems** – Analyze performance metrics, recognition, and hiring criteria. Do they support or undermine emotionally intelligent behavior?

3. **Engage stakeholders** – Partner with HR, DEI, and senior leadership to share audit insights and align on next steps.

4. **Pilot a shift** – Choose one area (e.g., onboarding, manager training, performance reviews) and embed EI explicitly into its design.

5. **Measure and iterate** – Track outcomes such as psychological safety, trust scores, or engagement, and refine your approach accordingly.

You don't need to redesign everything at once. Start with one layer. Build momentum.

Conclusion: Culture Is the Curriculum

The most powerful leadership development doesn't stop at the individual level. It redefines the environment in which those leaders grow.

When emotional intelligence is embedded in systems, rituals, and norms, it becomes an integral part of how an organization operates, makes decisions, and leads.

Culture becomes the curriculum. Leaders become the message.

A Transition to What's Next

To build organizations that scale, emotionally intelligent leadership must be designed into the conditions that allow it to take root.

That responsibility increasingly falls to learning and development.

In the next chapter, we explore the emerging role of T&D as transformation architect—shifting from content delivery to system design, and from isolated learning events to immersive, organizational transformation.

11

The Role of T&D in the Age of AI

"We're Not Just Teaching Skills Anymore. We're Shaping the Soul of the Organization."

When a senior T&D leader at a global logistics firm was tasked with launching an "AI-readiness" program, she expected technical upskilling to be the central challenge.

Instead, she encountered fear.

Employees weren't just asking how to use AI. They were asking:

- *Will I still matter?*
- *What's my value now?*
- *Am I being replaced?*

So she changed course. She launched a series of emotionally intelligent learning sessions on resilience, adaptability, and self-awareness. Only after addressing the human experience did she introduce the tools.

"Once they felt seen as people," she reflected, "they could learn as professionals."

This shift illustrates a broader truth. In the machine age, the most effective learning and development (T&D) functions won't just teach content. They'll hold space for complexity, for humanity, and growth.

T&D as a Transformation Catalyst

In a world reshaped by AI and continuous disruption, organizations don't just need faster learners. They need deeper leaders. Leaders who can think clearly in chaos, act with integrity under pressure, and connect across differences—not just to manage change, but to lead through it.

That's why the role of T&D is evolving. In this moment, learning and development isn't just about transferring skills. It's about guiding transformation. T&D is being called to serve as a transformation catalyst—an engine for personal growth, cultural renewal, and organizational adaptability.

The Shift in T&D's Role: From Content Provider to Catalyst

In the Age of AI, the core responsibilities of T&D are shifting dramatically:

- **From delivering information** to **facilitating identity-level growth**

- **From one-size-fits-all programs** to **curated, emotionally resonant experiences**

- **From tracking completions and hours** to **measuring behavior change and cultural impact**

- **From supporting the business** to **co-architecting its future**

- **From isolated skill-building** to **integrated, human-centered development ecosystems**

To be a transformation catalyst is to go beyond upskilling. It means designing learning environments that shift mindsets, reshape behaviors, and realign identity with purpose. It's not about what learners remember after a session—it's about who they become because of it.

The first frontier of this work is leadership development. AI is accelerating the pressure on leaders to do more with less, to move faster with fewer certainties. But leadership in this age isn't just about speed, it's about emotional steadiness.

Talent and development leaders are uniquely positioned to shape organizational culture and accelerate the success of the organization through the leadership development programs they design and deliver, with EI embedded into every aspect of those programs. Programs that forge emotionally intelligent leaders who remain calm and grounded when the storm of transformation and market turmoil is raging around them

Yet transformation doesn't stop at the top. T&D must also help leaders foster emotional intelligence within their teams through manager enablement initiatives, peer coaching circles, and facilitated reflection practices. These micro-cultures of trust and psychological safety can become the building blocks of a broader cultural shift. As emotionally intelligent behaviors take root in one team, they ripple outward.

To create durable change, T&D must then look upstream—partnering across the organization to embed emotional intelligence into the operating system. This means aligning policies, processes, and platforms to reinforce the leadership and relational behaviors we want to sustain.

Cross-Functional Collaboration for Embedding EI

Partner Function	How T&D Collaborates to Embed Emotional Intelligence
HR / People Ops	Co-design performance management, promotion, and succession planning systems that value relational skills and psychological safety.
IT / Technology	Integrate EI readiness into AI rollouts; pair digital training with emotional adaptation initiatives.
Operations	Align leadership behaviors with frontline realities; ensure emotionally intelligent practices scale across levels and geographies.
DEI / Employee Experience	Reinforce inclusive culture through empathy-driven onboarding, storytelling, and recognition systems.
Executive Leadership	Align strategic vision with emotionally intelligent leadership modeling and cascade messaging.

In this broader role, T&D becomes the connective tissue of the organization, aligning leadership behavior, team experience, and cultural systems around a shared human foundation.

This is the work ahead. To move from delivering content to cultivating capacity. From enabling performance to sustaining transformation. From being seen as a support function to being valued as a strategic partner.

T&D is no longer just delivering training. It's shaping the conditions for leadership that lasts. In the age of AI, where technology advances rapidly and trust develops slowly, the most strategic thing any organization can do is invest in its people. The most powerful partner in that effort is you.

From Slide Decks to Soul Work

Most leadership training still centers on the delivery of information, including decks, tools, and frameworks. But as the demands on leaders grow more complex, the learning must deepen.

T&D must now ask: Are we building programs that actually change people?

Soul work doesn't mean being sentimental or soft. It means creating conditions where leaders:

- Confront their internal narratives

- Reflect on their emotional triggers

- Build the self-awareness needed to act with integrity under pressure

To move from slide decks to soul work, T&D practitioners should:

- **Open with story, not theory** – Design sessions that begin with lived experiences, not just learning objectives. Start with a personal reflection, case study, or shared dilemma that grounds the work in human experience.

- **Integrate emotional check-ins** – Build in structured moments where participants pause and name what they're feeling. This can range from a simple one-word opener to in-depth journaling prompts tied to identity.

- **Create space for discomfort** – Allow time for silence. Don't rush to fill gaps with content. Transformation often emerges from tension, not resolution.

- **Model vulnerability** – Facilitators should be trained to lead with authenticity, not authority. When they share from their own experiences, it invites participants to go deeper.

The goal is not to cover more content—it's to uncover more truth. That's how leaders grow. That's how organizations change.

Five Principles of Transformational Program Design

From research and practice, five principles consistently support identity-level transformation:

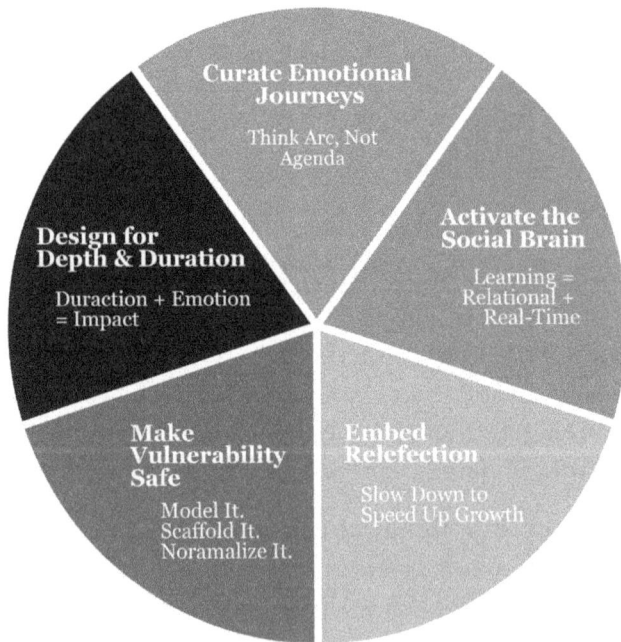

1. **Depth and Duration** – Short bursts don't change behavior. Sustained experiences allow emotional depth, reflection, and integration. Learning needs rhythm, not just reach.

2. **Emotional Journey Design** – Transformation follows an emotional arc: initial disruption → discomfort → deeper reflection → identity reconstruction → reengagement. T&D must map this journey intentionally, designing sessions with emotional pacing.

3. **Psychological Safety** – According to Amy Edmondson's research, learners will not take emotional risks without a sense of safety. No vulnerability, no growth. Programs must foster norms that encourage honest dialogue, acknowledge imperfection, and accept discomfort.

4. **Structured Reflection** – Insight requires pause. Reflection should be designed into the experience, not left to chance. Think prompts, journaling, peer discussions, and guided debriefs.

5. **Social Activation** – Learning deepens through community. Peer challenge, group coaching, and cohort-based formats accelerate growth by making learning a relational experience.

These aren't instructional preferences. They're transformation strategies.

What This Means for Leadership Development

To rise to this moment, T&D must:

- Design for identity transformation, not just skill development

- Normalize emotional intelligence as strategic, not supplemental

- Prioritize experience over efficiency

- Own the human edge as a competitive advantage

T&D professionals are now:

- **Curators of transformative experiences**, designing spaces that reveal, not just inform

- **Cultural architects**, shaping what leadership looks and feels like

- **Capability architects**, integrating EI into the fabric of the organization

- **Bridge builders**, helping transform the future of work by unlocking human potential

- **Stewards of the human edge**, advocating for the capacities that keep us uniquely human

Opportunity for Reflection

- Are you delivering information—or catalyzing transformation?

- Are your programs emotionally resonant—or merely efficient?

- How are you shaping identity, not just instruction?

Practice for T&D Leaders

Host a strategy sprint with HR, DEI, and Technology leaders. Use a cross-functional lens to map key AI-driven changes facing your workforce in the next 6–18 months. Then:

1. Identify the emotional and relational capabilities required to meet those changes.

2. Assess your current learning offerings—what builds those capabilities? What doesn't?

3. Prioritize learning experiences that support adaptability, empathy, and identity stability during times of disruption.

4. Co-create a roadmap that embeds emotionally intelligent learning into onboarding, manager development, and change readiness initiatives.

Use these questions to guide your roadmap:

- What future behaviors will leaders need to embody?

- How are those behaviors practiced, modeled, and reinforced today?

- Where are your cultural or systems gaps—and who must you partner with to close them?

Conclusion: T&D as a Strategic Force for Human Leadership

In a world racing toward automation, human capacity becomes the most valuable asset.

That's T&D's charge:

- **Architects of transformation**

- **Stewards of emotional culture**

- **Champions of leadership who feel, connect, and create meaning**

AI may shape the tools. But T&D will shape the people who use them.

That makes your role not just relevant, but irreplaceable.

A Transition to What's Next

Transformation doesn't count unless it lasts.

In the next chapter, we'll explore how to measure what matters—not just completions or smile sheets, but real indicators of impact:

- Observable behavioral change

- Team and cultural shifts

- Tangible business outcomes

Because the question isn't: *Did they enjoy it?*
It's: *Did it work?*

12

Measuring What Matters— Evaluating Impact and ROI

"It Wasn't Just My Leadership That Changed. It Was My Relationships, My Confidence, My Team."

When Tina returned from an eight-week immersive leadership program, her direct reports noticed something before she did.

She gave clearer direction, but also paused to listen more intently. She focused on tasks, but held space for emotion. Her presence felt different—steadier, more empathetic, more grounded. Her team began showing up differently as well. Collaboration increased. Friction decreased. Her peers began asking what she had done differently. Her sponsor took notice.

"I went for leadership development," Tina reflected. "What I found was a new way to relate to others—and myself."

So, how do we measure that?

How do we evaluate growth that's emotional, behavioral, and cultural, not just instructional?

Why Traditional Metrics Fall Short

When it comes to measuring the impact of investments in developing emotionally intelligent leaders, most organizations still rely on metrics designed for a bygone era—one focused on knowledge transfer, rather than identity transformation. Learning dashboards often highlight:

- Training completions

- Learning hours logged

- Quiz scores

- Post-training satisfaction surveys

While easy to capture, these indicators reflect activity rather than impact. They indicate whether someone attended a program or retained surface-level knowledge, rather than whether their behavior changed, their mindset evolved, or their team dynamics improved.

This gap becomes even more glaring when developing emotionally intelligent leaders. Traditional methods rarely tell us:

- *Did the leader become more self-aware under stress?*

- *Do team members feel safer, more heard, or more engaged?*

- *Has feedback become more candid, compassionate, and productive?*

- *Are inclusive behaviors being practiced, not just discussed?*

The Kirkpatrick Model—still widely used—was never designed to capture identity-level or emotionally driven change. While it provides a helpful baseline, most organizations stop at Level 1 (reaction) or Level 2 (learning). Rarely do they track Level 3 (behavior) or Level 4 (results), especially for emotionally intelligent competencies.

As one T&D leader shared: "We were measuring who liked the session. What we really needed to know was who led differently because of it."

Why This Matters in the Age of AI

AI is accelerating change at a rate that is faster than most organizations can absorb. McKinsey reports that 50% of current work activities could be automated with existing technology, yet only a fraction of companies feel prepared for the people side of this shift.

This technological disruption is fueling:

- Uncertainty about roles and job security

- Anxiety about skills obsolescence

- Resistance to AI-driven tools perceived as impersonal or biased

- Emotional fatigue from constant transformation initiatives

The fear isn't just technical—it's existential. People are asking, "Where do I fit in a future shaped by machines?"

Leaders play a crucial role in answering that question. Their ability to respond with empathy, clarity, and courage has a direct impact on morale, retention, and engagement. But without emotionally intelligent leadership, the result is often mistrust, disengagement, or quiet quitting.

Gartner's 2024 research indicates that emotionally intelligent leaders are 2.6 times more likely to retain high-performing teams during periods of transformation. Deloitte found that organizations that prioritize human capabilities during AI rollouts see up to 30% higher success rates in digital transformation initiatives.

In short, the cost of not measuring EI isn't just missed development—it's also missed retention, innovation, and trust.

What Changes When Leaders Change

Emotionally intelligent leadership is not soft—it's system-shaping. It's visible in behaviors that ripple through meetings, decisions, and team dynamics.

Let's compare the before and after of leadership transformation:

Leadership Behavior	Traditional Approach	Emotionally Intelligent Approach	Observable Impact
Communication	Top-down, informational	Dialogic, empathetic	Increased psychological safety
Conflict Resolution	Avoidance or escalation	Curiosity and calm	Faster recovery from tension
Decision-Making	Efficiency-driven, siloed	Values-driven, inclusive	Broader buy-in and more resilient outcomes
Team Engagement	Transactional	Relational and trust-based	Higher engagement and discretionary effort
Feedback Culture	Infrequent, critical	Regular, compassionate, and two-way	Stronger performance and growth mindset
Change Management	Directive	Supportive, with emotional scaffolding	Less burnout and greater adaptability
Inclusion	Policy-oriented	Practiced through daily micro-behaviors	Increased belonging and retention

One program participant summed it up this way: "My team didn't respond to what I told them to do. They responded to how I made them feel safe enough to speak up."

That kind of shift doesn't just change the tone of a team—it changes outcomes across the business. From retention and engagement to innovation and customer satisfaction, emotionally intelligent leadership drives measurable performance. Here are just a few key indicators that reflect its impact:

1. **Employee Retention and Turnover Rates**

   o **Why it matters:** High EQ leaders foster psychological safety and a sense of belonging, which in turn reduces voluntary attrition.

   o **How to track:** Compare turnover data pre- and post-intervention in teams with emotionally intelligent managers.

   o **Example:** Teams with emotionally intelligent leaders see turnover reductions of 20–40% (Deloitte, HBR).

2. **Employee Engagement Scores**

   o **Why it matters:** EI leaders are better at motivating, listening, and aligning purpose, core drivers of engagement.

   o **How to track:** Use Gallup Q12, CultureAmp, or similar tools to monitor engagement before and after leadership development.

   o **Example:** Emotionally intelligent leaders consistently score higher on "My manager cares about me as a person" metrics.

3. **Team Productivity and Goal Attainment**

   o **Why it matters:** Leaders who build trust and manage conflict well enable higher-performing, more collaborative teams.

o **How to track:** Evaluate business unit productivity, project delivery timelines, or OKR completion rates.

o **Example:** Google's Project Aristotle found psychological safety (an EI outcome) as the #1 predictor of team success.

4. **Psychological Safety Index**

o **Why it matters:** Teams led by emotionally intelligent leaders feel safer speaking up, sharing ideas, and taking risks.

o **How to track:** Include a 3–5 item psychological safety pulse in employee surveys.

o **Example:** Use Edmondson's scale or a similar, validated tool to measure perceptions of safety over time.

5. **Inclusion and Belonging Metrics**

o **Why it matters:** EI fosters empathy and inclusive behavior, critical for retention and performance in diverse teams.

o **How to track:** Use DEI dashboards, participation in ERGs, and inclusion-focused survey items.

o **Example:** Leaders trained in inclusive feedback and active listening drive a 3–to 5–fold increase in underrepresented employee engagement (McKinsey).

6. **Leadership Bench Strength and Internal Promotions**

o **Why it matters:** Developing emotionally intelligent leaders ensures more promotable, agile talent within the org.

o **How to track:** Track internal mobility, bench readiness scores, and succession plan coverage.

o **Example:** Organizations with robust EI training promote from within at significantly higher rates (LinkedIn Workplace Learning Report).

7. **Customer Satisfaction (CSAT/NPS)**

   o **Why it matters:** Teams that are engaged, aligned, and led well deliver better customer experiences.

   o **How to track:** Cross-reference customer satisfaction scores with the leadership EQ of internal service teams.

   o **Example:** Companies that focus on EI leadership development often see an NPS lift of 10–20 points (Forrester).

8. **Conflict Resolution Timelines or Escalation Frequency**

   o **Why it matters:** EI leaders de-escalate, listen well, and mediate effectively, reducing time lost to internal friction.

   o **How to track:** Track conflict-related HR cases or employee relations interventions before/after interventions.

9. **Innovation or Idea Generation Metrics**

   o **Why it matters:** EI environments increase trust and openness, which are precursors to innovation.

   o **How to track:** Number of new ideas submitted, design thinking participation, hackathon engagement.

   o **Example:** High psychological safety (rooted in EI leadership) correlates with a 3x increase in innovation outcomes (Google).

10. **Manager Effectiveness Scores**

   o **Why it matters:** Manager ratings (via surveys or skip-levels) offer clear feedback on leadership quality and EI.

   o **How to track:** Collect upward feedback regularly on qualities such as empathy, communication, and supportiveness.

From Metrics to Meaning

In a quarterly business review, the CHRO of a global tech firm was asked to prove the ROI of an immersive leadership program.

She didn't start with slides. She started with stories:

- A leader who helped their team navigate layoffs with transparency and trust

- A senior manager who reported their first-ever positive 360 feedback after shifting from control to curiosity

- A department that saw engagement scores jump 18% after peer coaching circles were introduced

Then she shared the numbers:

- 22% drop in turnover

- 12% lift in customer satisfaction

- Faster team recovery after an acquisition

"ROI is real," she said. "But it starts with how people feel—and what that makes possible."

The room nodded. Because they'd felt it too.

Opportunity for Reflection

- Are we measuring attendance or impact?

- Are our programs tracking emotional capacity, or just information recall?

- What would we see if we asked, "Who are our leaders becoming?"

Practice for T&D Leaders

To begin measuring the impact of emotional intelligence—at both the individual and organizational levels—T&D must design with intentionality. Here's how:

1. Define the Outcomes That Matter

- Identify 3–5 emotionally intelligent behaviors tied to your business goals (e.g., resilience, inclusive feedback, conflict recovery).

- Use these to set clear, measurable objectives for leadership programs.

2. Build Mixed-Method Evaluation Tools

- Use a blend of:

  o 360° feedback loops

  o Self-reflection journals

  o Manager and team check-ins

  o Sentiment analysis from engagement surveys

  o Coaching session logs

3. Measure Over Time, Not Just at the End

- Use lightweight pulse checks at 30, 60, and 90 days post-program to capture sustained behavior.

4. Collaborate Across the Org

- Partner with:

    o HR to align behavior change with promotion and performance systems

    o DEI to track inclusive leadership outcomes

    o IT to integrate feedback tools into the flow of work

    o People Analytics to connect EI growth to engagement, trust, and attrition metrics

5. Tell the Story of Transformation

- Complement your data with human stories. Capture leader narratives of change and team reflections on culture shifts. These stories turn metrics into meaning.

Conclusion: Redefining ROI

In the old model, ROI meant: "Did they complete the course?"

In today's world, it must ask: "Did this experience help leaders grow in ways that matter to our people, our culture, and our future?"

That's the shift:

- From instruction to evolution

- From reaction to resilience

- From knowledge gained to trust built

The organizations that measure what emotionally intelligent leadership enables—not just what it teaches—will be the ones best prepared to lead through AI, uncertainty, and everything that comes next.

A Transition to What's Next

Now that we've explored how to measure what matters, it's time to step back and look at the whole picture.

The final chapter is not a summary. It's a threshold.

It brings together the big ideas—the why, the how, and the what now—into a vision for the future of leadership and the role we all play in shaping it.

Because developing emotionally intelligent leaders isn't just a program. It's a movement.

13

Forging a New Paradigm of Leadership Development

"We don't need more content. We need more courage."

For decades, leadership development followed a familiar formula: build competence, deliver curriculum, track completions. It worked—for a time. But today's landscape is different. The disruptions aren't episodic; they're systemic. The pressure on leaders isn't just to perform but to transform amid ambiguity, moral tension, and accelerating change driven by AI and automation.

Leadership in the age of AI isn't just about driving results. It's about holding space for uncertainty, making values-based decisions in morally gray areas, and guiding teams through emotional terrain machines can't navigate. This new reality demands a new paradigm.

From Transfer to Transformation

Traditional leadership development programs assume that knowledge transfer leads to behavioral change. But when the learning need is emotional intelligence or broad behavioral change, transfer falls short. These aren't skills you can download—they're *forged through experience*.

Transformational learning theory (Mezirow, 1991) shows that deep change occurs when individuals critically examine their assumptions, experience emotional dissonance, and engage in reflective dialogue. EI development follows a pattern that requires a journey blending experience, self-awareness, and social learning.

What this means for T&D:

- Swap passive consumption for active, immersive learning.

- Replace "best practice" with "identity practice."

- Build the courage to disrupt comfort zones and design for emotional truth.

From Competencies to Capabilities

Competency models still matter, but they're not enough. In emotionally charged environments, capability matters more than checklists. A leader might "demonstrate conflict resolution" on paper, yet fail to defuse a real conflict if they lack self-regulation or empathy.

Capabilities are integrated and lived. They reflect not just what a leader knows, but who they are becoming. They draw from Kolb's experiential learning cycle: concrete experience → reflective observation → abstract conceptualization → active experimentation.

What this means for T&D:

- Shift the focus from skills to states of being.

- Develop assessment tools that track growth in presence, adaptability, and self-awareness.

- Make room for failure, feedback, and narrative transformation.

From Individual Growth to Systemic Shift

You can't grow emotionally intelligent leaders in a culture that rewards control, suppresses emotion, or penalizes vulnerability. Even the most powerful leadership program will fail if it returns leaders to environments where emotional intelligence is not a priority.

Organizations must evolve their operating systems—culture, structures, and incentives—to reinforce EI. T&D becomes the systems integrator, working across functions to align policies, rituals, and leadership expectations with emotionally intelligent behavior.

What this means for T&D:

- Partner with HR to embed EI into performance reviews and promotion criteria.

- Collaborate with DEI teams to reinforce inclusion and belonging.

- Align with senior leaders to role-model and signal the value of emotional competence.

From Learning Events to Development Ecosystems

EI isn't mastered in a one-day seminar. It requires space, repetition, feedback, and time. Think in ecosystems—not events.

Longitudinal learning, coaching, cohort-based dialogue, and workplace application must interweave. Tools like developmental feedback loops, narrative journaling, and emotional intelligence coaching (supported by reflective supervision) enable sustained transformation.

What this means for T&D:

- Use program scaffolding: pre-work, immersion, reflection, peer support, and post-program integration.

- Design for a learning rhythm—development that evolves alongside daily work.

- Treat identity development as the long arc of leadership.

From Content Creators to Experience Architects

In this new paradigm, T&D becomes a catalyst for transformation, not a content library. That means designing emotionally resonant experiences that awaken, stretch, and sustain growth.

This includes:

- Immersive challenges that activate the emotional brain (not just the cognitive one).

- Peer forums that hold space for reflection and growth.

- Learning rituals that anchor identity shifts over time.

As one senior facilitator shared: "I used to teach. Now I curate environments where leaders meet themselves more honestly."

Practice for T&D Leaders

Use this reflective practice to begin your shift: Identify one existing leadership program currently focused on knowledge transfer.

- What is the emotional journey of the participant?
- Where is there an opportunity for identity exploration?
- How can peer accountability and emotional activation be added?
- What tools will support ongoing behavioral rehearsal?

Then, reframe the program's goal from "teaching leadership skills" to "forging emotionally intelligent leaders who model the culture you want to scale."

An Invitation to Act

This book wasn't meant to share theory. It was written to equip you for action.

As a T&D leader, you're not just building leadership development programs—you're shaping the culture leaders carry into every room they walk into. You're designing experiences that influence how people make decisions, build trust, and show up in moments that matter.

The age of AI has made your role even more critical. As technology advances at a rapid pace, your role is to help people slow down and make thoughtful choices. As complexity grows, your job is to create clarity. As automation accelerates, your job is to keep humanity at the center of leadership and culture.

This isn't about being perfect. It's about being intentional. Choosing to design for transformation, not just content delivery. Choosing to embed emotional intelligence into the fabric of leadership development programs, not as a module, but at the core.

The tools are here, the research is clear, the need is urgent, the question now is: What will you build?

APPENDICES

A Chapter-by-Chapter Reflection

This summary distills the core insights, research themes, and practitioner takeaways from each chapter of Forging Emotionally Intelligent Leaders in the Age of AI. Whether you're a T&D professional designing transformative programs, an executive coach guiding leaders through identity-level change, or a senior leader embedding EI into your culture, this section offers a quick-reference guide to the book's most actionable insights. Each entry captures not only what the chapter covers, but also the key takeaways.

Chapter 1: The Moral Frontier of Leadership in the Age of AI

AI is not just a technical revolution—it's a moral and ethical minefield. Emotional intelligence helps leaders navigate ambiguity with empathy and integrity.

Practitioner Takeaways:

- Position emotional intelligence (EI) as a leadership imperative, not a soft skill.

- Frame AI readiness not only around skill-building, but around ethical and emotional grounding.

- Use moral complexity as an entry point for reflective leadership practice.

Chapter 2: When Machines Think Faster, Leaders Must Feel Deeper

The speed of AI requires a depth of humanity. Leaders must shift from transactional management to relational leadership.

Practitioner Takeaways:

- Design programs that help leaders slow down and leverage emotional intelligence competencies under pressure.

- Integrate reflection practices that foster inner stillness amidst external volatility.

- Help leaders surface their emotional narratives, not just master cognitive tools.

Chapter 3: The Problem With Traditional Leadership Development

Critiques the "training-as-transfer" model and argues for immersive, identity-based learning.

Practitioner Takeaways:

- Replace one-off events with longitudinal experiences.

- Design for depth and duration to produce effective behavioral change and identity shift.

- Prioritize developmental readiness and emotional engagement.

Chapter 4: The Neuroscience of Leadership Transformation

Transformation occurs when the brain is safe, engaged, and rewired through emotional experiences.

Practitioner Takeaways:

- Design for neuroplasticity: integrate safety, emotion, and feedback over time.
- Avoid cognitive overload—less content, more connection.
- Use emotional disruption as a catalyst, not a breakdown.

Chapter 5: Designing Programs That Transform

Programs must be designed with a growth arc and identity-based goals.

Practitioner Takeaways:

- Build emotional arcs into program design: safe entry → challenge → reflection → integration.
- Simulate real-world tension to accelerate growth.
- Sequence feedback and identity work intentionally to avoid overwhelm.

Chapter 6: Safe Containers and the Deep Work of Identity Transformation

Psychological safety is the foundation for vulnerability and change.

Practitioner Takeaways:

- Prioritize safety before content.

- Create rituals and norms that reward vulnerability.

- Train facilitators to hold emotional space, not just deliver material.

Chapter 7: The Power of Peer Dynamics and Cohort-Based Learning

Peer relationships and cohort dynamics accelerate insight and reinforce identity shifts.

Practitioner Takeaways:

- Build programs around consistent cohort interaction.

- Use peer feedback to enhance behavioral awareness.

- Design group norms that foster trust and challenge.

Chapter 8: The Immersive Advantage & Why Duration Matters

Sustained, immersive experiences produce deeper, longer-lasting transformation.

Practitioner Takeaways:

- Opt for multi-week or longer program durations and integration periods to drive transformation.

- Design for emotional sequencing, not just content sequencing.

- Pair immersion with coaching and peer dialogue.

Chapter 9: Coaching, Dialogue, and Living the Insights Forward

Coaching and reflection embed growth into daily practice and foster sustainable transformation.

Practitioner Takeaways:

- Integrate coaching as a bridge from learning to action.

- Use journaling and reflective dialogue as a scaffolding tool.

- Encourage post-program accountability structures.

- Equip coaches to work with identity, not just performance.

Chapter 10: Embedding Emotional Intelligence into Organizational DNA

Emotionally intelligent organizations model, reinforce, and reward EI systemically to create a sustainable strategic advantage.

Practitioner Takeaways:

- Treat EI as a collective capability, not just an individual trait.

- Integrate EI into hiring, feedback, promotion, and performance reviews.

- Elevate emotionally intelligent leaders as cultural signalers and stewards of emotionally intelligent microcultures.

- Embed EI into strategic language and leadership expectations.

- Measure and model emotionally intelligent behavior at every level.

Chapter 11: The Role of T&D in the Age of AI

T&D must design emotionally resonant learning experiences, human-centered cultures, and become catalysts for ongoing organizational transformation.

Practitioner Takeaways:

- Redefine T&D's role from course creators to transformation designers.

- Design for belonging, reflection, and identity evolution.

- Bridge technical change with human growth.

Chapter 12: Measuring What Matters— Evaluating Impact and ROI

Traditional metrics fall short. T&D must capture behavioral, emotional, and cultural impact.

Practitioner Takeaways:

- Shift from "did they like it?" to "did they become someone new?"

- Blend qualitative stories with quantitative performance indicators.

- Link emotional intelligence to strategic business outcomes, such as retention, trust, and innovation.

Chapter 13: Forging a New Paradigm of Leadership Development

Leadership development must evolve from instruction to transformation, from events to ecosystems, from competence to identity.

Practitioner Takeaways:

- Rethink leadership development as a systemic, identity-shaping, organizational transformation practice.

- Position T&D as stewards of emotional culture and transformation.

- Lead the movement toward more human, more emotionally intelligent leadership.

References

Chapter 1: The Moral Frontier of Leadership in the Age of AI

Boyatzis, R. E., & McKee, A. (2005). *Resonant leadership: Renewing yourself and connecting with others through mindfulness, hope, and compassion.* Harvard Business Review Press.

Goleman, D. (1995). *Emotional intelligence: Why it can matter more than IQ.* Bantam.

Boyatzis, R. E., Goleman, D., & Rhee, K. (2000). Clustering competence in emotional intelligence. In R. Bar-On & J. D. A. Parker (Eds.), *The handbook of emotional intelligence* (pp. 343–362). Jossey-Bass.

Goleman, D., Boyatzis, R., & McKee, A. (2002). *Primal leadership: Realizing the power of emotional intelligence.* Harvard Business Review Press.

Boyatzis, R. E. (2006). Intentional change theory from a complexity perspective. *Journal of Management Development, 25*(7), 607–623. https://DOI.org/10.1108/02621710610678445

Goleman, D. (2017). What makes a leader? *Harvard Business Review.* https://hbr.org/2004/01/what-makes-a-leader

World Economic Forum. (2023). *Future of jobs report 2023.* https://www.weforum.org

McKinsey & Company. (2023). *The state of organizations 2023.* https://www.mckinsey.com

Pew Research Center. (2023, May 24). *How Americans view artificial intelligence.* https://www.pewresearch.org/short-reads/2023/05/24/how-americans-view-artificial-intelligence/

Six Seconds. (2021). *State of the heart: 2021 emotional intelligence trends.* https://www.6seconds.org/2021/03/30/state-of-the-heart-2021/

Deloitte. (2020). *A new era for customer engagement: The rise of purpose-led brands.* Deloitte Insights. https://www2.deloitte.com/insights/us/en/industry/retail-distribution/global-marketing-trends.html

Sellers, M. D. (2024). *A study of the efficacy of multi-week, immersive, experiential, in-person executive education programs for developing emotional intelligence competencies in senior executives as perceived leadership effectiveness* (Publication No. 31331580) [Doctoral dissertation, University of Pennsylvania]. ProQuest Dissertations & Theses.

Chapter 2: When Machines Think Faster, Leaders Must Feel Deeper

Goleman, D. (1998). *Working with emotional intelligence.* Bantam.

Boyatzis, R. E. (2018). *The competent manager: A model for effective performance.* John Wiley & Sons.

Cherniss, C. (2010). Emotional intelligence: Toward clarification of a concept. *Industrial and Organizational Psychology, 3*(2), 110–126. https://doi.org/10.1111/j.1754-9434.2010.01231.x

Goleman, D., Boyatzis, R. E., & McKee, A. (2002). *Primal leadership: Realizing the power of emotional intelligence.* Harvard Business Review Press.

Sellers, M. D. (2024). *A study of the efficacy of multi-week, immersive, experiential, in-person executive education programs for developing emotional intelligence competencies in senior executives as perceived leadership effectiveness* (Publication No. 31331580) [Doctoral dissertation, University of Pennsylvania]. ProQuest Dissertations & Theses.

Chapter 3: The Problem With Traditional Leadership Development

Kolb, D. A. (1984). *Experiential learning: Experience as the source of learning and development.* Prentice Hall.

Brinkerhoff, R. O. (2006). *Telling training's story: Evaluation made simple, credible, and effective.* Berrett-Koehler.

Sellers, M. D. (2024). *A study of the efficacy of multi-week, immersive, experiential, in-person executive education programs for developing emotional intelligence competencies in senior executives as perceived leadership effectiveness* (Publication No. 31331580) [Doctoral dissertation, University of Pennsylvania]. ProQuest Dissertations & Theses.

Chapter 4: The Neuroscience of Leadership Transformation

Mezirow, J. (1991). *Transformative dimensions of adult learning.* Jossey-Bass.

Brookfield, S. D. (2013). *The skillful teacher: On technique, trust, and responsiveness in the classroom.* Jossey-Bass.

Siegel, D. J. (2010). *The mindful therapist: A clinician's guide to mindsight and neural integration.* W. W. Norton & Company.

Sellers, M. D. (2024). *A study of the efficacy of multi-week, immersive, experiential, in-person executive education programs for developing emotional intelligence competencies in senior executives as perceived leadership effectiveness* (Publication No. 31331580) [Doctoral dissertation, University of Pennsylvania]. ProQuest Dissertations & Theses.

Chapter 5: Designing Programs That Transform

Dirksen, J. (2015). *Design for how people learn* (2nd ed.). New Riders.

Van Velsor, E., McCauley, C. D., & Ruderman, M. N. (2010). *The Center for Creative Leadership handbook of leadership development* (3rd ed.). Jossey-Bass.

Sellers, M. D. (2024). *A study of the efficacy of multi-week, immersive, experiential, in-person executive education programs for developing emotional intelligence competencies in senior executives as perceived leadership effectiveness* (Publication No. 31331580) [Doctoral dissertation, University of Pennsylvania]. ProQuest Dissertations & Theses.

Chapter 6: Safe Containers and the Deep Work of Identity Transformation

Brown, B. (2018). *Dare to lead: Brave work. Tough conversations. Whole hearts.* Random House.

Schein, E. H. (2013). *Humble inquiry: The gentle art of asking instead of telling.* Berrett-Koehler.

Sellers, M. D. (2024). *A study of the efficacy of multi-week, immersive, experiential, in-person executive education programs for developing emotional intelligence competencies in senior executives as perceived leadership effectiveness* (Publication No. 31331580) [Doctoral dissertation, University of Pennsylvania]. ProQuest Dissertations & Theses.

Chapter 7: The Power of Peer Dynamics and Cohort-Based Learning

Hazan, C., & Shaver, P. R. (1987). Romantic love conceptualized as an attachment process. *Journal of Personality and Social Psychology, 52*(3), 511–524. https://doi.org/10.1037/0022-3514.52.3.511

Kegan, R. (1994). *In over our heads: The mental demands of modern life.* Harvard University Press.

Kegan, R., & Lahey, L. L. (2016). *An everyone culture: Becoming a deliberately developmental organization.* Harvard Business Review Press.

Johnson, S. M. (2008). *Hold me tight: Seven conversations for a lifetime of love.* Little, Brown.

Wenger, E. (1998). *Communities of practice: Learning, meaning, and identity.* Cambridge University Press.

Sellers, M. D. (2024). *A study of the efficacy of multi-week, immersive, experiential, in-person executive education programs for developing emotional intelligence competencies in senior executives as perceived leadership effectiveness* (Publication No. 31331580) [Doctoral dissertation, University of Pennsylvania]. ProQuest Dissertations & Theses.

Chapter 8: The Immersive Advantage & Why Duration Matters

Petriglieri, G. (2020). F**k leadership. *Academy of Management Learning & Education, 19*(2), 249–265. https://doi.org/10.5465/amle.2019.0283

O'Neil, D. A., & Marsick, V. J. (2007). Understanding action learning. In M. Pedler (Ed.), *Handbook of action learning* (pp. 3–26). Palgrave Macmillan.

Sellers, M. D. (2024). *A study of the efficacy of multi-week, immersive, experiential, in-person executive education programs for developing emotional intelligence competencies in senior executives as perceived leadership effectiveness* (Publication No. 31331580) [Doctoral dissertation, University of Pennsylvania]. ProQuest Dissertations & Theses.

Chapter 9: Coaching, Dialogue, and Sustaining the Change

Boyatzis, R. E. (2018). *Helping people change: Coaching with compassion for lifelong learning and growth.* Harvard Business Review Press.

Rogers, C. R. (1961). *On becoming a person: A therapist's view of psychotherapy.* Houghton Mifflin.

Sellers, M. D. (2024). *A study of the efficacy of multi-week, immersive, experiential, in-person executive education programs for developing emotional intelligence competencies in senior executives as perceived leadership effectiveness* (Publication No. 31331580) [Doctoral dissertation, University of Pennsylvania]. ProQuest Dissertations & Theses.

Chapter 10: Embedding Emotional Intelligence into Organizational DNA

Goleman, D. (2013). The focused leader. *Harvard Business Review*. https://hbr.org/2013/12/the-focused-leader

Senge, P. M. (2006). *The fifth discipline: The art and practice of the learning organization*. Doubleday.

Sellers, M. D. (2024). *A study of the efficacy of multi-week, immersive, experiential, in-person executive education programs for developing emotional intelligence competencies in senior executives as perceived leadership effectiveness* (Publication No. 31331580) [Doctoral dissertation, University of Pennsylvania]. ProQuest Dissertations & Theses.

Chapter 11: The Role of T&D in the Machine Age

Birkman, R. (2022). The new era of learning and development: How AI is shaping the T&D function. *Training Journal*.

Deloitte. (2023). *2023 Global human capital trends report*. https://www2.deloitte.com

Sellers, M. D. (2024). *A study of the efficacy of multi-week, immersive, experiential, in-person executive education programs for developing emotional intelligence competencies in senior executives as perceived leadership effectiveness* (Publication No. 31331580) [Doctoral dissertation, University of Pennsylvania]. ProQuest Dissertations & Theses.

Chapter 12: Measuring What Matters— Evaluating Impact and ROI

Kirkpatrick, D. L., & Kirkpatrick, J. D. (2006). *Evaluating training programs: The four levels* (3rd ed.). Berrett-Koehler.

Phillips, J. J., & Phillips, P. P. (2016). *The value of learning: How organizations capture value and ROI and translate them into support, improvement, and funds.* Wiley.

Sellers, M. D. (2024). *A study of the efficacy of multi-week, immersive, experiential, in-person executive education programs for developing emotional intelligence competencies in senior executives as perceived leadership effectiveness* (Publication No. 31331580) [Doctoral dissertation, University of Pennsylvania]. ProQuest Dissertations & Theses.

Chapter 13: Forging a New Paradigm of Leadership Development

Petriglieri, G. (2020). The return of existential learning. *Academy of Management Learning & Education, 19*(2), 278–285. https://doi.org/10.5465/amle.2019.0320

Wheatley, M. J. (2006). *Leadership and the new science: Discovering order in a chaotic world* (3rd ed.). Berrett-Koehler.

Sellers, M. D. (2024). *A study of the efficacy of multi-week, immersive, experiential, in-person executive education programs for developing emotional intelligence competencies in senior executives as perceived leadership effectiveness* (Publication No. 31331580) [Doctoral dissertation, University of Pennsylvania]. ProQuest Dissertations & Theses.

A Field Guide for Practitioners

A Starting Point, Not a Prescription

This Field Guide is designed to help facilitators, T&D professionals, executive coaches, and organizational leaders bring the ideas from *Forging Emotionally Intelligent Leaders in the Age of AI* to life through practice.

Rather than presenting a linear or prescriptive curriculum, this guide offers a flexible, experience-driven toolkit organized by the stages of a leadership development program—from early design through measurement and post-program momentum.

Each activity includes practical metadata (when to use it, how long it takes, group size, and materials) as well as guidance grounded in adult learning theory. Whether you're building a six-month cohort journey or integrating emotional intelligence into a single workshop, these exercises are intended to support deeper learning, identity development, and sustained behavioral change.

Use this guide as a design companion.

Adapt it to your organizational culture, learners, and market context.

Let safety, resonance, and transformation—not convenience—be your compass.

The most powerful learning experiences aren't flawless.

They're real, human, emotionally alive, and courageously held.

Program Design Phase

These exercises are designed to help T&D professionals, instructional designers, and transformation leaders build emotionally intelligent leadership development programs from the ground up. They support emotional pacing, values alignment, and systemic reinforcement before the first session even begins.

Emotional Arc Mapping

Best For: Designing full program architecture

Time Required: 60–90 minutes

Group Size: 2–10 (T&D design team, facilitators, or program architects)

Materials: Whiteboard or digital canvas (e.g., Miro, MURAL), markers or sticky notes, printed timeline templates

Purpose: To design emotionally resonant learning journeys that build psychological safety, intensity, insight, and integration across the program lifecycle.

Instructions:

1. Map the program timeline (hour-by-hour, day-by-day, or weekly, depending on program structure). Identify key touchpoints, including kickoff events, immersion activities, peer coaching, and capstone moments.

2. For each segment, define the intended emotional tone (e.g., curiosity, tension, vulnerability, clarity, celebration).

3. Sequence the experiences to ensure proper rhythm—balancing stretch and support, activation, and integration.

4. Adjust timing or flow to allow space for emotional processing, group cohesion, and applied reflection.

Facilitator Notes:

- Emotional pacing matters more than the volume of content.

- Include reflective or grounding practices after emotionally intense experiences.

- Use this mapping as a guide during facilitation, not a rigid schedule.

Facilitator Reflection:

- Did our emotional arc align with the leadership transformation we aim to support?

- Where might the sequence create overwhelm or stagnation?

- How can we better balance emotional activation with safety and space?

Paradigm Shift Canvas

Best For: T&D team visioning and program redesign

Time Required: 60–75 minutes

Group Size: 4–12 (T&D leads, facilitators, program architects)

Materials: Large canvas (physical or digital), quadrant template, sticky notes or markers

Purpose: To identify outdated leadership development assumptions and generate bold, future-aligned design experiments grounded in emotional intelligence.

Instructions:

1. Create a canvas with four labeled quadrants:

   o What We've Outgrown

   o What We're Becoming

   o What We're Afraid to Let Go

   o What We're Ready to Try

2. Invite participants to reflect silently and add ideas to each quadrant.

3. Facilitate discussion around shared themes, tensions, or inspiration.

4. Identify 1–2 bold, low-risk experiments to pilot in the next program cycle.

5. Revisit the canvas quarterly to track what has shifted or emerged.

Facilitator Notes:

- Normalize tension between letting go and innovating.

- Use story or metaphor to deepen exploration.

- Embrace discomfort as a cue for transformation.

Facilitator Reflection:

- What beliefs or routines did we struggle to release?

- Where did energy and enthusiasm emerge?

- How can we cultivate experimentation as a habit, rather than a one-time act?

Organizational Emotional Intelligence (EI) Audit

Best For: Cross-functional alignment around systems that support or hinder emotionally intelligent leadership

Time Required: 90 minutes

Group Size: 6–15 participants (HR, T&D, DEI, Operations, senior leaders)

Materials: Audit template, flip charts or virtual boards, data on organizational culture

Purpose: To assess whether organizational systems and processes reinforce the emotional intelligence competencies being taught in leadership development programs.

Instructions:

1. Choose 3–5 systems to review, such as:

    o   Hiring and onboarding

    o   Manager training

    o   Performance reviews

    o   Promotions and succession planning

    o   Team communication rituals

2. For each system, ask:

    o   Does this system reinforce emotional intelligence behaviors?

    o   Where are the disconnects between stated values and actual practices?

3. Brainstorm 1–2 small shifts per system to better support EI-aligned leadership.

4. Assign owners for each change and commit to a 90-day follow-up.

Facilitator Notes:

- Use anonymized stories or case examples to illustrate pain points.

- Keep the focus on small, doable shifts.

- Frame the conversation around culture stewardship, not compliance.

Facilitator Reflection:

- What assumptions about "how we do things" were surfaced?

- Where are we unintentionally undermining the impact of our leadership development efforts?

- What systems feel most ready for small, high-leverage change?

Measurement & Feedback

These exercises help T&D practitioners assess, document, and communicate the impact of emotionally intelligent leadership development. They prioritize behavioral evidence, narrative signals, and practical tools to support continuous improvement and organizational alignment.

Training-as-Transfer Audit

Best For: Program evaluators reviewing or redesigning leadership initiatives

Time Required: 45–60 minutes

Group Size: T&D teams or program designers

Materials: Audit worksheet, flip charts, or digital workspace

Purpose: To evaluate whether current leadership development programs are designed for transformation, not just content delivery.

Instructions:

1. Identify 2–3 existing leadership programs.

2. For each, assess:

   o Are learners emotionally engaged?

   o Does the experience include reflection or identity work?

   o Are peer dynamics and feedback loops present?

   o Is a real-world application embedded into the flow?

3. Identify missing elements (e.g., coaching, somatic practice, psychological safety).

4. Sketch a redesigned version with experiential, emotional, and social learning integrated.

Facilitator Notes:

- Use the "Fallacy of Training-as-Transfer" section from Chapter 4 as a discussion primer.

- Focus redesigns on inclusion, pacing, and sustained reflection, not more content.

Facilitator Reflection:

- What assumptions did we surface about what counts as "learning"?

- Which redesign ideas felt most promising or uncomfortable?

- What cultural factors may support or resist this shift?

Define & Detect Transformation Workshop

Best For: Strategic program planning and stakeholder alignment

Time Required: 90–120 minutes

Group Size: Cross-functional team of HR, T&D, business unit leaders

Materials: Outcome framework templates, pulse survey samples, dashboards

Purpose: To help organizations define what transformation looks like—and how to detect it using both data and stories.

Instructions:

1. Facilitate a working session to answer:

   o What are our top 3–5 transformation goals?

   o What observable behaviors or moments reflect those goals?

   o What signals can we track at the individual, team, and system levels?

2. Choose a data collection mix (e.g., interviews, peer feedback, behavior-based metrics).

3. Build a sample storytelling dashboard or simple impact scorecard.

4. Discuss how to share these stories internally for learning and accountability.

Facilitator Notes:

- Encourage teams to include "moments that matter" (turning points, breakthroughs) as evidence, not just quantitative metrics.

- Frame this as an ongoing listening strategy, not a one-time evaluation.

Facilitator Reflection:

- What resistance did I observe around nontraditional metrics?

- Which stories or signals created the most energy in the group?

- How can I incorporate transformational storytelling into future programs?

Design for Duration Audit

Best For: Redesigning or optimizing long-term learning experiences

Time Required: 45 minutes

Group Size: Talent and development leaders

Materials: Program calendars, integration plan templates

Purpose: To assess whether programs are structured to support long-term leadership growth and integration of emotional intelligence.

Instructions:

1. Review the timeline and components of 1–2 current programs.

2. Evaluate for:

   o Length and spacing between sessions

   o Emotional pacing across the arc

   o Integration points (coaching, peer support, action planning)

3. Identify gaps (e.g., front-loaded content, lack of practice windows).

4. Draft an enhanced program arc with:

   o One immersive or emotionally engaging component

   o A 60–90 day follow-up loop

   o Peer or coaching support for integration

Facilitator Notes:

- Challenge the assumption that shorter is better.

- Use evidence from the book's case studies to support longitudinal design.

Adult Learning Theory Anchor:

Spacing effect and integration—real transformation takes time, support, and reinforcement.

Facilitator Reflection:

- Did this audit reveal quick wins or long-term redesign needs?

- Where does our current culture support or resist extended learning journeys?

- How might I advocate more persuasively for program duration?

Insight-to-Action Protocol

Best For: Post-session follow-through and accountability

Time Required: 15–30 minutes

Group Size: Any size

Materials: Sticky notes, digital tracker, or commitment wall

Purpose: To support the translation of emotional and cognitive insight into specific, trackable behavior change.

Instructions:

1. At the end of a session or module, ask:

   o "What resonated emotionally with you today?"

   o "What will you commit to doing differently as a result?"

2. Have participants write insight–action pairs on sticky notes or a shared board.

3. Schedule a follow-up touchpoint 2–3 weeks later (peer circle, coaching, or pulse check).

4. Reflect: What supported action? What created friction?

Facilitator Notes:

- Normalize that change takes time.

- Invite peer affirmation and support for each commitment.

- Consider showcasing some actions anonymously as a "Commitment Wall."

Facilitator Reflection:

- Did participants write specific and meaningful commitments?

- How many followed through, and what helped?

- How might I evolve this into a regular design element?

Program Launch & Conclusion

These foundational and closing practices help learners explore who they are as leaders, anchor the program in values and presence, and leave with commitments that extend well beyond the classroom.

Personal Leadership Ethos Statement

Best For: Program kickoff, values clarification, identity work

Time Required: 60 minutes

Group Size: Individual with small group reflection

Materials: Journals, reflection guide handouts

Purpose: To help leaders clarify their values, ethical commitments, and sense of moral presence in complex environments.

Instructions:

1. Reflect on a leadership moment that tested emotional or ethical clarity.

2. Journal using prompts:

   o What values conflicted?

   o What emotions surfaced?

   o How did I respond, and what does it reveal?

3. Write a brief ethos statement addressing:

   o "What do I believe about leadership under pressure?"

o "What do I stand for when others are impacted by my decisions?"

4. Share in small groups or dialogue circles.

Facilitator Notes:

- This is about reflection, not performance.

- Revisit the ethos statement later in the program to note how it evolves.

Facilitator Reflection:

- How open were participants to exploring moral complexity?

- What shifts did I observe in tone or vulnerability during sharing?

Who Am I as a Leader? Narrative Identity Exercise

Best For: Mid-program reflection, identity development

Time Required: 60–75 minutes

Group Size: Pairs, then whole-group debrief

Materials: Journals, optional storycards

Purpose: To surface unconscious leadership narratives and support identity evolution through storytelling.

Instructions:

1. Provide journaling prompts:

o Who taught me to lead?

o When did I betray or uphold my values?

o What part of me rarely shows up in leadership?

2. Silent writing (10 minutes)

3. Paired storytelling shares (5 minutes each)

4. Optional: storyboard "The Leader I Am Becoming"

5. Group debrief on themes, discomforts, and insights

Facilitator Notes:

- Use a grounding ritual to open.

- Model storytelling by going first.

- Normalize discomfort—it often signals a breakthrough moment.

Facilitator Reflection:

- What emotions or breakthroughs surfaced?

- How did the room shift from before to after the exercise?

Embodied Presence Practice

Best For: Any session requiring emotional regulation or grounding

Time Required: 30–45 minutes

Group Size: Any

Materials: Breathwork script, quiet space, optional music

Purpose: To help leaders regulate emotions and build presence in moments of stress or pressure.

Instructions:

1. Begin with a guided somatic practice: breathwork, grounding, or body scan.

2. Introduce a leadership scenario or stressor.

3. Run a brief role-play or visualization.

4. Pause and ask:

   o What emotions are surfacing?

   o Where do you feel them?

5. Re-run the scenario with grounded awareness.

Facilitator Notes:

- Use trained guides for deeper somatic work.

- Debrief not just the scenario, but the body's response.

Facilitator Reflection:

- What did participants learn from their body's response?

- How might we build somatic awareness into other parts of the program?

Memory-Making Leadership Moments

Best For: Mid-to-late program reflection, transition planning

Time Required: 60–75 minutes

Group Size: Individuals, then pairs, then small groups

Materials: Journals, storyboard templates

Purpose: To reflect on defining emotional leadership moments, and design future moments aligned with purpose.

Instructions:

1. Journal about a defining leadership moment:

   o What happened?

    o   What emotions surfaced?

    o   How did it shape who I am?

2. Share in pairs or trios.

3. Co-design a future moment: storyboard or describe a moment you want to create.

4. Debrief in small groups.

Facilitator Notes:

- Use after trust is built.

- Guide the group to notice emotional themes, not just outcomes.

Facilitator Reflection:

- How clearly were emotions tied to impact?

- Did this exercise shift participants' future vision or commitment?

Final Note to Practitioners

This guide is a flexible framework, not a fixed formula.

Emotional intelligence is not taught through lecture. It's discovered through insight, emotion, and relationship. As a practitioner, your job isn't to perform content. It's to create the conditions for transformation: safety, curiosity, tension, and truth.

Each exercise here is a doorway. Enter boldly, reflect often, and hold space for what emerges. Your presence, your design choices, and your trust in the learner's capacity will shape what's possible.

You are not just building leaders.

You are designing the future of work—one emotionally intelligent decision, moment, and program at a time.

Would you like a cleanly formatted version of this complete Field Guide for manuscript integration?

About the Author

Dr. Mikah D. Sellers is a nationally recognized workforce futurist, leadership strategist, and award-winning educator with over two decades of experience guiding organizations through digital transformation, executive development, and cultural change. He has served as Chief Innovation Officer, Chief Digital Officer, and senior advisor across Fortune 500 companies, government agencies, and venture-backed startups—helping leaders navigate complexity at the intersection of human potential and emerging technology.

Mikah earned his doctorate in Organizational Leadership and Learning from the University of Pennsylvania, where his research explored how immersive, multi-week, experiential executive education programs can build emotional intelligence competencies in senior leaders and foster lasting behavioral change. He also holds an MBA from NYIT, as well as multiple master's degrees in communication and education, and executive credentials from the Wharton Advanced Management Program and the McCombs School of Business.

As a long-time faculty member at Georgetown University's School of Continuing Studies, Mikah taught the Capstone in Technology Management and was honored with the university's prestigious Tropaia Award for Outstanding Faculty. His teaching blended practice-based curriculum development, experiential learning, and executive coaching to develop emotionally intelligent, practice-ready leaders.

His leadership work has been recognized with W3 Awards, PR Daily honors, and a REBRAND 100 Award. Beyond accolades, Mikah's passion lies in helping leaders cultivate the emotional intelligence and ethical courage needed to lead humanely and effectively in an increasingly AI-driven world.

His debut book, *Forging Emotionally Intelligent Leaders in the Age of AI*, provides a blueprint for designing transformative learning experiences that support identity evolution, foster relational trust, and achieve lasting impact in a time of unprecedented disruption.

Acknowledgements

This book marks the culmination of a journey that began long before a single word was written. It is the product of years spent studying, listening, facilitating, and reflecting—shaped by the many people who walked alongside me with wisdom, encouragement, and belief.

To my mentors—Dr. Annie McKee, Dr. Matthew Lippincott, and Dr. Raghu Krishnamoorthy—thank you for your candor, insight, and unwavering support. Each of you challenged me to think more deeply, challenge assumptions, push boundaries, and write with purpose. This work is stronger because of your guidance.

To the extraordinary leaders who participated in my research: your honesty, vulnerability, and lived experience gave this book its heartbeat. You trusted me with your stories, and I hope these pages do them justice.

To my peers and mentors in the Chief Learning Officer program at the University of Pennsylvania's Graduate School of Education: thank you for pushing me beyond knowledge toward impact. Your curiosity, intellect, and friendship shaped both the substance of this book and the spirit behind it.

To Susan, Cameron, and Peyten—thank you for your love, your patience, your support, and your belief in me. Through long nights and countless revisions, you never stopped encouraging me. Your support is the foundation that steadied me every step of the way.

To Erik Laubacher—friend, thought partner, and unofficial editor—thank you for reading far too many drafts, always with generosity and insight. Your presence was a gift throughout this process.

To my former students at Georgetown University, especially those in the Capstone Course for the Master's in Technology Management: teaching you was one of the greatest honors of my professional life. Your drive to lead with both technological fluency and human integrity continues to inspire me. I remain deeply grateful to have been recognized with the Tropaia Award for Faculty Member of the Year, a reflection of your brilliance, not mine.

Finally, to every learning and development professional, executive coach, or leader I've had the privilege of working with throughout my career: thank you for doing the hard, human work of leadership. This book is for you. May it equip and encourage you to forge the emotionally intelligent leaders the future needs.

Join the Movement

This book isn't just a collection of ideas—it's a call to reimagine leadership development for a new era.

As AI reshapes how we work, technical skill alone is no longer enough. We need emotionally intelligent leaders—those who can navigate uncertainty, build trust across differences, and foster human connection in the face of constant change.

That kind of leadership doesn't emerge by accident. It's cultivated by practitioners like you: learning designers, executive coaches, educators, and practitioners who are ready to move beyond outdated models and create meaningful, identity-shaping experiences.

We've reached the edge of what information transfer can accomplish. What comes next is transformation—rooted in emotional intelligence, fueled by immersion, and sustained through connection.

This is your invitation to lead that shift.

What You Can Do Now

1. **Bring These Ideas Into Your Practice:** Infuse emotional intelligence into how you teach, coach, and lead. Use the field guide. Run the exercises. Adapt and evolve them. Let practice—not just theory—drive your work.

2. **Convene Your Community:** Transformation is relational. Start conversations. Host a book circle. Facilitate a peer cohort. Build a community of practice dedicated to human-centered leadership in the age of AI.

3. **Redesign the Experience:** Audit your programs. Ask bold questions: Are we moving hearts, not just minds? Are we building containers for growth, not just delivering content? Are we inviting and enabling people to transform, not just to perform?

4. **Share What Works:** Make your insights visible. Post reflections. Host a session. Write the case study. Help build the collective wisdom of what emotionally intelligent leadership looks like—when done well, and with intention.

5. **Stay Connected:** Visit www.mikahsellers.com for downloadable tools, facilitation templates, and details about upcoming workshops and community gatherings. Join a growing network of practitioners advancing this work.

The Work Ahead

Forging emotionally intelligent leaders isn't a trend. It's a necessity. It's about reclaiming leadership as a human act, rooted in courage, presence, and care.

No single book, facilitator, or program will make this shift alone. But together—through shared purpose and deliberate design—we can shape what leadership becomes.

Let's build what comes next.
Let's lead like it matters.
Let's forge a new era of emotionally intelligent leadership—together.

www.ingramcontent.com/pod-product-compliance
Lightning Source LLC
Chambersburg PA
CBHW031502180326
41458CB00044B/6666/J